Customer Care Chronicles:Navigating Difficult Interactions with Ease

Mastering the Art of Customer Service

David Thompson

Table of Contents

INTRODUCTION

In the field of customer service, dealing with consumers can frequently bring up difficulties that call for dexterity, understanding, and skill to resolve. Service professionals need to be prepared with the skills and strategies to handle challenging interactions with professionalism and ease, whether they are handling a complaint, settling a dispute, or handling high-stress situations. "Customer Care Chronicles: Navigating Difficult Interactions with Ease: Mastering the Art of Customer Service" is a thorough manual for service providers who want to flourish in their positions by handling difficult situations and providing outstanding customer care.

Being the first point of contact between a company and its clients, customer service is an essential part of any business. Therefore, maintaining positive relationships with customers, fostering loyalty, and boosting business performance are all dependent on having the poise and expertise to handle difficult circumstances. Giving service workers the skills, knowledge, and strategies they need to thrive in today's competitive world is the goal of this book.

The relevance of empathy in customer service encounters is examined at the outset of the trip. Comprehending the viewpoint, feelings, and requirements of the client and reacting with empathy entails being kind and perceptive. Even under challenging circumstances, service providers can develop rapport, win consumers' trust, and forge meaningful connections by practising empathy. Gaining proficiency in the art of customer service also requires active listening and efficient communication. In order to completely comprehend the worries and expectations of the customer, service personnel need to practice active listening. Furthermore, timely and efficient information transmission, issue resolution, and conflict resolution all depend on clear and succinct communication.

Another essential quality this book explores is resilience. Managing unanticipated obstacles, dealing with challenging clients, and negotiating high-stress scenarios are all everyday tasks in customer service positions. Service providers may remain composed under pressure, recover from setbacks, and stay committed to providing outstanding customer experiences by cultivating resilience.

Moreover, culture and organizational support are essential for promoting service excellence. Organizations must prioritize training and development programs, devote resources to skill upgrading, and foster a culture that supports and fosters continuous learning and growth. Establishing a friendly and encouraging work environment for service personnel can help firms increase customer happiness, loyalty, and, eventually, economic success.

In conclusion, "Customer Care Chronicles: Navigating Difficult Interactions with Ease: Mastering the Art of Customer Service" is an extensive guide for service professionals looking to improve their abilities and handle difficult situations with assurance and competence. In today's cutthroat business world, service professionals can create unforgettable client experiences that propel their organizations to success by embracing empathy, communication, resilience, and ongoing learning.

CHAPTER I

Understanding Customer Behavior

Types of Difficult Customers

Being able to handle challenging clients is not only a necessary ability in the field of customer service, but it also demands mastery. Every client engagement has a particular set of challenges, and by knowing the many kinds of challenging customers, service providers can be better equipped to handle these interactions with grace and elegance. Organizations may provide their frontline personnel with the necessary tools and techniques to transform potentially harmful experiences into chances for positive engagement and long-lasting pleasure by understanding the underlying motivations and behaviours of different customer types.

An example of a typical kind of challenging client is the "Angry Customer." These people frequently enter interactions already irritated or frustrated, whether because of a perceived lack of attention, a problem with a product or service, or outside circumstances beyond the company's control. Anger can take many forms, such as raised voices or aggressive words, and dealing with angry clients necessitates striking a careful balance between aggressiveness and understanding. Rebuilding trust and reducing stress can be accomplished by listening to their worries, sincerely apologizing, and acting quickly to address them.

An additional difficult client category is the "Indecisive Customer." These people have trouble making decisions, frequently as a result of ignorance or anxiety over choosing the incorrect option. Being unable to make a decision can result in drawn-out conversations, heightened frustration, and unhappiness for both the client and the service provider. When providing indecisive consumers with assistance, service providers should be patient, attentive to their needs, and able to make recommendations that are tailored to their priorities and preferences. Service providers can assist customers in developing trust and confidence in their decisions by confidently and reassuringly guiding them through the decision-making process.

On the other hand, the "Entitled Customer" poses a distinct set of difficulties. These people feel that because of their perceived status or brand devotion, they should receive preferential treatment or benefits. Demanding behaviour, irrational demands, and a feeling of superiority over service personnel are some examples of entitlement. It takes strict boundaries, open lines of communication, and an emphasis on justice and equity to handle entitled clients. While trying to satisfy customers' wants while adhering to company policy and ethical standards, service personnel must resist giving in to irrational demands.

Service providers may also run into the "Manipulative Customer," who uses strategies like guilt-tripping, threats, or deceit to get what they want. Customers who are manipulative may try to take advantage of compassion or empathy in order to influence the service provider's choices or demand concessions that go beyond what is practical or reasonable. It is imperative to identify deceptive strategies and preserve a professional distance when interacting with these clients. It is essential for service professionals to maintain objectivity, adhere to corporate regulations, and refrain from succumbing to emotional manipulation or compulsion.

In addition, the "Impatient Customer" is a typical obstacle in hectic settings where people anticipate instant satisfaction. These people are intolerant of waiting periods, delays, or obstacles in the way of the process, and they frequently voice their annoyance or displeasure with what they perceive to be inefficiencies. Proactive communication, efficiency, and transparency are necessary when handling impatient customers. To reduce annoyance and avoid escalations, service providers need to emphasize promptness, set reasonable deadlines, and actively manage expectations.

Finally, the "Uninformed Customer" can have trouble if they don't know enough about certain goods, services, or procedures. These people could ask the same questions over and over again, look for explanations for simple ideas, or show uncertainty about complex subjects. It takes time, clarity, and education to serve ignorant clients properly. Service providers need to break down complex ideas into manageable chunks, deliver pertinent information in easily assimilated ways, and provide support and advice based on the comprehension level of the client.

In summary, the ability to effortlessly navigate challenging conversations is a critical competency for customer service representatives. Service workers may turn unpleasant interactions into chances for positive engagement and long-term client pleasure by knowing the different kinds of problematic customers and using the right strategies and techniques. Mastering the art of customer service and developing strong relationships with customers, improving brand loyalty, and propelling corporate success require a combination of empathy, patience, assertiveness, and professionalism.

Psychological Factors at Play

Knowledge clients' external behavior is not enough to navigate challenging relationships with them; you also need to have a knowledge of the psychological aspects involved. In our book "Navigating Difficult Interactions with Ease: Mastering the Art of Customer Service," we explore the intricate interactions between feelings, perceptions, and thought processes that affect how customers behave.

Emotions are one of the main psychological variables at work in consumer encounters. Customers' perceptions of and reactions to their experiences are greatly influenced by their emotions. While negative emotions like anger and irritation can result in complaints and discontent, positive emotions like happiness and contentment can boost advocacy and loyalty. To handle challenging interactions with clients effectively, customer service representatives need to be sensitive to their emotional states and respond with empathy, a key element that makes them invaluable in our operations.

Perception is another crucial psychological component. Consumers' expectations and behaviour might be influenced by how they view a scenario or encounter. Because perception is subjective, a person's personal prejudices, cultural background, and prior experiences can all have an impact. In order to prevent misunderstandings and misinterpretations, customer service representatives should be aware of how their actions and communication may be interpreted by clients. They should also make an effort to maintain clarity and transparency.

Customer interactions are significantly influenced by cognitive processes as well. Consumers use cognitive functions, including memory, attention, and decision-making, to manage their business relationships and make wise decisions. Nonetheless, their behaviour and decision-making may be influenced by cognitive biases and limits. Customers may, for instance, be influenced by confirmation bias to look for information that supports their own assumptions or ideas or by anchoring bias to place an undue emphasis on first impressions or information. Customer care representatives can anticipate and handle customer concerns more skillfully if they are aware of these cognitive biases.

Moreover, social variables have a big impact on consumer behaviour. Consumers may be swayed in their decision-making or experience evaluation by peer pressure, social comparison, and social standards. Furthermore, other people's presence—whether it be in person or virtually—can affect how clients act and communicate with one another. To successfully manage challenging conversations, customer service personnel, with their unique position and skills, need to be aware of these social factors and modify their approach accordingly, empowering them to handle any situation with confidence.

Furthermore, it is crucial to take the idea of power dynamics into account while interacting with customers. The unequal allocation of power among people or groups is referred to as power dynamics, and it can affect how those people or groups interact. Power dynamics can appear in a variety of ways in customer service interactions. For example, customers may hold power because of their purchasing power, or workers may have power because of their knowledge and experience. By striking a balance between assertiveness, empathy, and respect, customer service professionals can handle challenging conversations more skillfully by having a better understanding of power relations.

In summary, managing challenging client encounters necessitates a thorough comprehension of the psychological aspects involved. Customer behaviour and the results of customer interactions are shaped by a variety of elements, including emotions, perceptions, cognitive processes, social factors, and power dynamics. Through the identification and management of these psychological elements, customer service representatives can improve their capacity to handle challenging situations with professionalism, efficacy, and empathy.

Empathy and Perspective-Taking

Empathy and the ability to see things from another person's point of view are critical abilities for establishing trusting bonds with clients and deftly managing challenging circumstances. The ability to empathize or put oneself in another person's shoes is a vital prerequisite for developing real connections and understanding the needs of clients. Additionally, by allowing service providers to view situations from several angles, perspective-taking broadens empathy and enhances their capacity to address issues comprehensively and compassionately.

Fundamentally, empathy is the ability to identify and comprehend the feelings, ideas, and experiences of other people. When it comes to customer service, this means paying attention to what consumers have to say, addressing their worries, and acting as though you genuinely care about them. Even in the face of difficulty, customer service workers may develop rapport, establish trust, and provide the groundwork for productive communication by empathizing with consumers.

However, in difficult or tense situations, empathy might not be enough on its own. This is where having a broad viewpoint comes in very handy. Beyond empathy, perspective-taking requires people to mentally recreate the emotions, motives, and thoughts of others. Service providers can better understand the root causes of client discontent or annoyance by accepting a variety of viewpoints, which opens the door to more focused and efficient remedies.

It takes expertise and experience to become an expert in the field of customer service, empathy, and perspective-taking. The development of emotional intelligence is necessary for service representatives if they are to become adept at both identifying and controlling their own feelings as well as those of others. They must also cultivate a sincere curiosity about the viewpoints and experiences of their clients in order to promote an atmosphere of respect and understanding.

The foundation of compassionate and perspective-taking relationships is effective communication. Service providers should use active listening strategies to make sure they fully understand the problems of their clients, such as paraphrasing and clarifying. They should also communicate with honesty, empathy, and clarity, giving clients the knowledge and assurances they require to feel respected and heard.

Empathy and perspective-taking are practical de-escalation techniques that reduce conflict and promote cooperation under challenging circumstances. Service agents can validate clients' emotions and start the process of rebuilding trust by showing empathy for their frustrations or concerns. At the same time, perspective-taking enables professionals to find points of agreement and investigate win-win alternatives, turning disagreements into chances for cooperation and settlement.

Furthermore, extending beyond encounters with customers, empathy and perspective-taking also extend to interactions within the organization. It is imperative that service executives cultivate a culture of compassion and perspective-taking by offering their people the necessary training, support, and direction to enable them. Leaders may foster an atmosphere where each team member feels appreciated, understood, and supported by setting an example of empathy and promoting candid communication.

To sum up, developing empathy and the ability to
see things from multiple angles are essential for being an expert in customer service. Service providers can create stronger bonds with clients, handle challenging situations with ease, and produce favorable results by developing these abilities. In the end, having the capacity to empathize and view the world from the perspective of others not only improves the client experience but
also strengthens the bonds of human connection by encouraging compassion, empathy, and understanding in all interactions.

CHAPTER II

Preparing Yourself for Difficult Interactions

Developing Emotional Intelligence

Emotional intelligence becomes a critical competency in the ever-changing world of customer care, enabling agents to handle difficult situations with grace and effectiveness. Empathy, self-control, self-awareness, and social skills are just a handful of the traits that comprise emotional intelligence. Certain qualities are necessary for both understanding and controlling one's own emotions as well as those of others. Enhancing their emotional intelligence can help service providers build stronger relationships with their clients, resolve issues more easily, and promote success even in the most trying circumstances.

Fundamental to emotional intelligence is self-awareness, or the capacity to identify and comprehend one's own feelings, assets, vulnerabilities, and stressors. Self-awareness is the cornerstone of effective communication and relationship-building for service professions. Service personnel can better control their reactions in difficult situations and keep their calm and professionalism even under duress by being aware of their own emotional responses. Furthermore, self-awareness helps people to see where they may improve themselves, which promotes perseverance in the face of difficulty and ongoing progress.

Self-regulation enables people to efficiently control their emotions and impulses, which is a complement to self-awareness. Self-regulation in the context of customer service means remaining emotionally stable and in control, even when provoked or hostile. Service providers need to be able to identify and accept their emotions without letting them control how they act. People who use techniques like deep breathing, mindfulness, and encouraging self-talk may control their feelings and handle challenging situations with poise and clarity.

Another essential component of emotional intelligence is empathy, which helps providers comprehend and relate to the feelings and experiences of others. Empathy in customer service means paying attention to what customers are saying, acknowledging their worries, and acting as though you genuinely care about them. Customer service professionals may establish connection, trust, and a spirit of cooperation by demonstrating empathy for their customers' ideas. Furthermore, empathy makes it possible for people to modify their responses to suit the particular requirements and preferences of every client, improving the overall quality of the service encounter.

Effective customer service requires a variety of skills, including teamwork, communication, and conflict resolution. These are all included in the category of social skills. To convey ideas effectively, sympathetically, and convincingly, service personnel need to have strong verbal and nonverbal communication skills. They must also be adept at resolving conflicts, calming heated situations, and coming up with solutions that work for all parties. Moreover, offering smooth and coherent service experiences requires teamwork and collaboration, especially in complicated or diverse interactions involving several stakeholders.

Self-reflection and deliberate practice are both necessary for the development of emotional intelligence. Service providers can improve their emotional intelligence in a number of ways, such as by asking for feedback, evaluating themselves, and continuing to learn and grow. People can learn important information about their emotional strengths and areas for development by thinking back on previous interactions and getting advice from peers and mentors. In addition, they can make use of resources, training courses, and workshops to learn new methods and abilities for boosting emotional intelligence in the context of customer service.

Being emotionally intelligent is not only a professional but also a moral need in the field of customer service. Regardless of the situation, service providers have an obligation to treat clients with empathy, decency, and respect. People may respect these values and make sure that every interaction is marked by professionalism, compassion, and honesty by developing their emotional intelligence. Additionally, emotional intelligence promotes inclusivity and fairness in the service experience by empowering professionals to handle obstacles like language limitations, cultural differences, and other difficulties with tact and understanding.

To sum up, mastering the art of customer service and smoothly navigating challenging conversations needs developing emotional intelligence. Enhancing self-awareness, self-control, empathy, and social skills can help service providers forge closer bonds with clients, diffuse tension, and promote favourable results. Emotional intelligence also helps companies create a culture of respect, empathy, and cooperation, which boosts worker morale, contentment, and retention. In the end, the key to providing excellent customer service is having the emotional intelligence and self-control to improve the lives of both clients and service providers.

Self-Regulation Techniques

Gaining control over one's emotions is essential for success in the customer service industry because it allows employees to handle difficult situations with poise, resiliency, and efficiency. The capacity to control one's feelings, inclinations, and reactions in a way that encourages productive dialogue, cultivates wholesome connections, and produces desirable results is known as self-regulation. Service providers who study and apply self-regulation techniques to maintain their professionalism and composure in the face of hardship can enhance the quality of the client experience and foster long-lasting customer loyalty.

The development of self-awareness, or the capacity to identify and comprehend one's own feelings, triggers, and behavioural patterns, is essential to the practice of self-regulation. Service providers need to become acutely aware of their emotional states and the variables influencing how they react in difficult circumstances. People can exert more control over their reactions and remain composed even in stressful situations by being aware of their emotions without letting them drive their actions. Furthermore, by being self-aware, caregivers can spot early indicators of growing emotions and take proactive measures to stop confrontations from getting worse.

By improving self-regulation, mindfulness can help service providers remain grounded, focused, and in the moment, even when dealing with demanding clients. In order to promote serenity and clarity, mindfulness is purposefully focusing attention on the current moment without passing judgment or feeling attached to it. People can develop inner peace and resilience by engaging in mindfulness practices like body scanning, deep breathing, and guided meditation. This will lessen the possibility that they will become overwhelmed or reactive under challenging circumstances. Additionally, mindfulness improves cognitive flexibility, which makes it easier for service workers to handle complex conversations and adjust more skillfully to unforeseen circumstances.

Another helpful tactic for controlling emotions and reinterpreting difficult circumstances in a more positive way is cognitive reappraisal. Cognitive reappraisal is the deliberate reevaluation of the relevance and meaning of a particular circumstance, with the goal of changing one's viewpoint to emphasize the opportunities rather than the threats. For instance, when a customer is not happy, customer care representatives might reframe the conversation as a chance to show empathy, problem-solving abilities, and dedication to customer pleasure.

Reframing obstacles as chances for development and education helps people develop a resilient and optimistic mindset that empowers them to handle challenging situations with self-assurance and resourcefulness.

Good communication abilities allow customer service representatives to express themselves succinctly, confidently, and sympathetically while staying aware of the requirements and feelings of their clients. These abilities are crucial for self-regulation in the industry. The goal of assertive communication is to respectfully and assertively communicate one's thoughts, feelings, and boundaries without using violence or passivity. Service providers can reduce the possibility of misunderstandings or confrontations by setting clear limits and expectations and then assertively stating their requirements and expectations. Furthermore, genuine empathy and understanding are shown by actively listening to clients, acknowledging their worries, and communicating with them in an empathic manner. Service providers can establish rapport, mutual respect, and trust by taking a sympathetic approach, which will encourage more positive and cooperative interactions with consumers.

An essential component of self-regulation is self-care, which allows service providers to refuel their bodies, minds, and spirits to maintain optimal health and performance. Exercise, good eating, rest, relaxation, and leisure activities are all critical components of self-care, which is what it means to be healthy and balanced when doing stressful customer service jobs. People can avoid burnout, improve resilience, and develop a sense of purpose and happiness in their work by making self-care a priority. Additionally, self-care helps service providers to approach client encounters with a fresh perspective, passion, and empathy, which improves the calibre of the customer and employee experience.

To sum up, self-regulation skills are not just essential for becoming an expert in customer service, but they also play a crucial role in shaping the client experience. Through the practice of self-awareness, mindfulness, cognitive reappraisal, assertive communication, and self-care, professionals in the service industry can improve their emotional resilience, remain composed, and promote favorable results even in the most trying situations. This fosters an environment of professionalism, ethics, and quality in businesses, which raises staff morale, contentment, and retention. The secret to providing outstanding customer service is ultimately emotional control, which not only improves the lives of service providers but also enhances the value and satisfaction of the clients they serve.

Building Resilience

Developing resilience appears to be an essential competency in customer service, enabling service providers to handle difficult situations with poise, flexibility, and efficiency. Resilience is the capacity to overcome hardship, recover from setbacks, and flourish in the face of adversity. Service workers who practice resilience are better equipped to handle stressful situations with poise, problem-solving skills, and emotional stability. This improves customer satisfaction and builds enduring client loyalty.

The development of a growth mindset—the conviction that obstacles and setbacks offer chances for development, learning, and self-improvement—is essential to developing resilience. Service providers need to have an optimistic, curious, and persistent mindset and see problems as transient rather than insurmountable. People can create a sense of resourcefulness and resilience by rephrasing obstacles as chances for personal growth and development. This will help them approach challenging situations with confidence and resilience.

In order for customer service professionals to effectively manage stress, regulate emotions, and preserve their well-being among the demands of their roles, they must develop adaptive coping techniques. Using habits and activities that enhance mental, emotional, and physical health—like exercise, mindfulness, relaxation techniques, and social support—are examples of adaptive coping strategies. Through proactive stress management and self-care, people can refuel their energy and resources, improving their ability to handle difficult situations with grace and efficacy.

Social support is essential as a defensive mechanism against the negative effects of stress and misfortune, enabling service providers to use the resources and encouragement of peers, mentors, and colleagues. There are several types of social support, including informational support (guidance, counsel), emotional support (empathy, listening), and instrumental support (assistance with duties). Creating strong bonds and relationships at work helps people feel more connected, supported, and camaraderie among themselves, which enhances resilience and general well-being.

Resilience is primarily shaped by optimism and positive thinking, which helps service workers stay upbeat and constructive even when faced with obstacles or disappointments. Those that are optimistic usually see obstacles as transient, focused, and controllable as opposed to persistent, all-encompassing, and unbeatable. People can stay motivated, persistent, and resilient by practising optimism, which helps them deal with challenging situations with resiliency and determination.

Flexibility and adaptability are critical traits for developing resilience in customer service, as they allow agents to accept change, adjust to shifting conditions, and deal with unforeseen difficulties in a productive manner. Being adaptable means having an open mind to fresh viewpoints, ideas, and methods in addition to being eager to try new things and gain experience. By exercising adaptability, people can develop a range of coping strategies and problem-solving tactics that will enable them to face difficult circumstances with courage, ingenuity, and agility.

Building resilience requires self-reflection and ongoing learning, which help service providers identify their areas of strength, weakness, and development. People might find areas for growth and development by thinking back on their previous experiences and getting input from mentors and coworkers. Furthermore, adopting a lifelong learning mentality helps people remain flexible, inquisitive, and receptive to fresh viewpoints, which strengthens their resilience and adaptability in the face of changing client demands and expectations.

To sum up, developing resilience is crucial to perfecting the art of customer service and smoothly handling challenging situations. Through the development of a growth mindset, adaptive coping mechanisms, social support, optimism, adaptability, self-reflection, and ongoing learning, professionals in the service industry can improve their ability to overcome obstacles, overcome setbacks, and prosper. Resilience also helps companies cultivate a culture of excellence, professionalism, and teamwork, which boosts employee happiness, morale, and retention. The ability to develop resilience is ultimately what makes excellent customer service possible, improving the lives of both clients and service providers.

CHAPTER III

Communication Strategies

Active Listening

Active listening is a fundamental ability in customer service that allows agents to interact with clients with effectiveness, empathy, and understanding. Active listening entails comprehending all of your customers' needs, wants, and worries and responding in a way that demonstrates your sincere concern for them. It goes beyond simply hearing what they have to say. Being adept at the art of active listening allows service providers to forge closer relationships with their clients, find solutions to issues, and encourage success even in the most difficult circumstances.

The ability to pay attention to the speaker without interruptions or distractions is essential to active listening. In order to facilitate active listening, service providers should reduce outside distractions and show that they are interested in the conversation by paying attention to their body language, which includes nodding, maintaining eye contact, and adopting an open sectionure. Customers can be encouraged to express themselves honestly and freely by receiving signals of attention and responsiveness from individuals. This helps establish the groundwork for productive dialogue and problem-solving.

A key element of active listening is empathy, which helps customer service representatives comprehend and relate to the feelings and experiences of their clients. In order to listen with compassion, one must pay attention to the speaker's underlying feelings, worries, and points of view in addition to what they are saying. Service providers can establish rapport, mutual respect, and trust with clients by acknowledging their feelings and exhibiting genuine understanding and concern. This promotes a sense of connection and collaboration.

One effective method for exhibiting empathy and confirming consumers' viewpoints is through reflective listening. Reflective listening entails summarizing and paraphrasing what clients have said in order to show empathy and verify understanding. Service providers can show that they are committed to comprehending and successfully meeting the demands of their clients by reiterating their concerns in their own words and acknowledging the feelings that underlie their communications. Reflective listening also helps clients feel heard and appreciated, which raises their level of satisfaction and confidence in the quality of the services they get.

Clarifying and probing are crucial elements of active listening that help support workers resolve ambiguities, obtain more details, and identify underlying issues or motives. Asking open-ended questions and requesting clarification when customers' statements are imprecise or confusing are two ways to clarify. Asking insightful inquiries and looking into the underlying motives or feelings of clients allows you to probe deeper into their worries. Service providers can make sure they have a thorough grasp of their client's wants and preferences by asking clarifying and probing questions. This will help them respond to customers more efficiently.

Active listening is greatly aided by nonverbal clues, which offer insightful information about the feelings, attitudes, and intentions of the people being observed. It is imperative for service personnel to closely observe nonverbal clues from consumers, including body language, gestures, and facial expressions, in order to assess their emotional condition and respond accordingly and accurately. People can improve rapport, empathy, and understanding, which will lead to more successful communication and problem-solving, by imitating the nonverbal signs of their clients and modifying their own communication style accordingly.

When used in conjunction with active listening, respectful silence may be a very effective strategy. It gives clients time to think, reflect, and clarify their ideas. In order to give clients the time and space to completely express their problems, service providers must fight the impulse to talk during every pause. By remaining silent with grace, people can show that they are patient, aware, and respectful of other people's space. This fosters an atmosphere that is accepting and judgment-free, which encourages candid dialogue and teamwork.

To sum up, active listening is essential to learning how to provide excellent customer service and smoothly handle challenging situations. By giving complete focus, exhibiting empathy, engaging in thoughtful listening, asking clarifying and probing questions, observing nonverbal clues, and accepting polite quiet, service providers can strengthen their relationships with clients, diffuse tension, and promote favourable results. Additionally, active listening helps companies develop a culture of understanding, empathy, and cooperation that boosts employee happiness, morale, and retention. At the end of the day, providing excellent customer service is all about having the ability to listen actively, which benefits both customers and service providers.

Effective Verbal and Nonverbal Communication

In order to manage challenging situations with grace, empathy, and competence, customer service professionals need to be able to communicate effectively if they are to succeed in the business. In this process, both spoken and nonverbal communication are essential for determining the nature of exchanges, promoting comprehension, and developing rapport with clients. Service providers can skillfully handle challenging circumstances, attend to client issues, and improve the entire service experience by developing their communication skills.

The spoken words, tone, and delivery that customer service representatives use to communicate with them are all considered forms of verbal communication. When communicating verbally, it's critical to be clear and succinct so that clients can understand and interpret your information with ease. Professionals providing customer service should speak clearly and avoid using technical jargon or terminology that could offend or confuse clients. In addition, they need to be mindful of the tone of their voice, making sure that it exudes professionalism, compassion, and empathy in order to build rapport and trust with clients.

Effective verbal communication requires active listening in order for service providers to fully comprehend the needs, feelings, and concerns that clients have to express. In addition to paying attention to what is being said, active listening entails sympathetically detecting the speaker's underlying feelings and intentions. Service providers can foster a supportive and cooperative atmosphere for meaningful conversation and problem-solving by actively listening and exhibiting attention to detail and empathy. In the end, this will raise the standard of the customer experience.

Nonverbal communication includes body language, gestures, facial expressions, and other nonverbal cues that convey emotions and information without the use of words. To ensure that communications are reliably and successfully transmitted, service providers need to be aware of both their own nonverbal signs and those of their clients. While negative nonverbal cues like frowning or crossed arms may indicate discomfort or indifference, positive nonverbal cues like smiling, nodding, and maintaining eye contact can improve rapport and trust. In client interactions, service providers can enhance their efficacy, clarity, and credibility by coordinating their verbal and nonverbal communication.

Effective communication requires both confirmation and clarity in order for service providers to be sure that their communications are correctly understood and received by clients. Restating or paraphrasing what customers have said in order to rectify any gaps or misunderstandings is known as clarifying. In order to ensure that consumers' requirements and expectations have been satisfied and to address any unanswered questions or concerns, confirmation entails asking for feedback from them. Service providers can avoid misunderstandings, settle disputes, and promote higher levels of satisfaction and trust in the service experience by providing clarification and confirmation.

Effective communication requires adaptability and flexibility, which allow customer service representatives to customize their approach to each individual's preferences and needs. In order to accommodate variations in personality, culture, and communication preferences, service personnel must be able to modify their communication style, vocabulary, and tone. In order to show their dedication to client satisfaction and ongoing development, businesses should also be prepared to alter their plans in response to criticism and evolving conditions. Service providers can improve their efficacy and resilience in handling challenging situations with ease by adopting adaptability and flexibility.

To sum up, mastering the art of customer service and resolving challenging situations with ease requires strong verbal and nonverbal communication skills. Service providers can develop rapport, establish trust, and promote positive outcomes in customer encounters by communicating effectively, showing empathy and active listening, observing nonverbal clues, and asking clarifying and affirming questions. In addition, proficient communication cultivates an environment of cooperation, compassion, and distinction in businesses, boosting staff morale, contentment, and retention. Effective communication is ultimately the foundation of excellent customer service, which improves the lives of both clients and service providers.

Clarifying and Confirming Understanding

In the context of customer service, the capacity to elucidate and verify comprehension is essential for promoting effective communication, settling disputes, and elevating the total client experience. Clarifying entails asking for more information or explanation to make sure that the wants, worries, and expectations of the customer are fully understood. Verifying that the consumer has appropriately received and understood the information provided by the service provider constitutes the process of confirming understanding. Service providers who are skilled at elucidating and verifying comprehension are able to establish favourable outcomes even in the most trying circumstances, foster trust, and handle complex relationships with ease.

Active listening enables service providers to become attuned to clients' issues, feelings, and preferences, which is the first step toward effective clarification. Carefully observing nonverbal indicators, tone of voice, and verbal cues allows service providers to spot areas of confusion or misunderstanding early on and make proactive clarification requests. Asking clarifying questions, like "Could you please elaborate on that?" or "Can you provide more details?" helps customer care representatives learn more and have a thorough grasp of the requirements and concerns of the customer. Additionally, you can ensure mutual understanding and help clients clarify their message by paraphrasing or restating their statements in their own terms.

In customer service encounters, it is equally crucial to confirm that the consumer has accurately received and interpreted the message that the service professional provided. Customer confirmation can be obtained directly from service providers through feedback requests, a summary of essential points, or other means. Phrases such as "Just to make sure I understand correctly..." or "Did I capture that correctly?", for instance, ask clients to explain or clear up any confusion, helping to avoid mistakes or misunderstandings. Service providers show their dedication to client pleasure and guarantee that clients' wants and expectations are successfully met by verifying comprehension.

In customer service contacts, nonverbal clues hold equal significance to spoken communication in terms of clarifying and verifying knowledge. Service providers must watch for body language, facial expressions, and other nonverbal clues to gauge whether a customer is understanding, engaged, and satisfied. Nonverbal indicators that are positive, like nodding, smiling, or maintaining eye contact, show understanding and agreement, whereas those that are negative, like scowling or crossing one's arms, could suggest misunderstanding or disagreement. Service providers can improve clarity and understanding in client encounters by harmonizing their verbal and nonverbal communication.

In customer service, skilful explanation and confirmation methods are critical for managing challenging conversations and settling disputes. While seeking clarification and confirming understanding, service personnel need to stay composed, patient, and empathic in difficult situations where emotions may run high or tensions may rise. The keys to reducing conflict and encouraging open communication with consumers are respect, empathy, and active listening. Building trust, repairing rapport, and finding mutually satisfying solutions to challenging interactions are all possible for service workers who validate clients' feelings, acknowledge their concerns, and show that they genuinely want to understand and meet their requirements.

Customer service representatives who want to get better at explaining and verifying what they understand must have access to feedback systems and ongoing improvement opportunities. Service providers can find areas for development and improve their communication efficacy by asking for feedback from clients, coworkers, or superiors. Furthermore, continuous training and development initiatives can give service providers the methods, strategies, and assets required to improve their communication abilities and handle challenging situations with assurance and competence. Service personnel can continually provide clients with excellent experiences and raise the calibre of their interactions by investing in ongoing learning and improvement.

To sum up, developing the skill of explaining and verifying knowledge is crucial to handling challenging situations with ease and becoming an expert in providing customer service. Service providers can promote clear communication, develop trust, and promote positive outcomes in customer encounters by actively listening, asking clarifying questions, and verifying understanding. Furthermore, by using efficient explanation and confirmation strategies, customer service representatives can lower stress, settle disputes, and improve customer satisfaction—all of which eventually boost the company's profitability and standing. In the end, providing excellent customer service is primarily about being able to clarify and validate understanding, which benefits both customers and service providers.

CHAPTER IV

De-escalation Techniques

Recognizing Signs of Escalation

Recognizing escalation signals is an essential skill for service personnel in the ever-changing world of customer support. Customer engagement reaches an escalation point when it becomes more stressful, confrontational, or emotionally charged, making it more challenging to communicate effectively and solve problems. Service providers can intervene proactively, defuse tension, and promote positive outcomes in even the most difficult conversations by becoming skilled at identifying symptoms of escalation.

Customers displaying increased emotional intensity is one of the primary indicators of escalation. This could show itself as a raised voice, irritation, or frustration in their body language or tone of speech. It is imperative for service personnel to be aware of these signs and to identify them as precursors of mounting stress. Service providers can ease tension and foster a more favourable atmosphere for productive conversation by empathetically and sympathetically acknowledging and validating their clients' emotions.

Repeated complaints or grievances from the customer are another indicator of an escalation. When clients express the same issues or complaints over and over again without feeling heard or understood, it may be a sign of growing annoyance or discontent. It is imperative that service providers actively and attentively listen to these concerns in order to show empathy and a sincere desire to fix the underlying problems. Service providers may stop issues from getting worse, prevent escalation, and win back customers' trust and happiness by addressing the underlying causes of complaints and offering prompt, practical remedies.

Elevating tension or frustration might also be indicated by changes in the customer's conduct or demeanour. For instance, in their dealings with service providers, clients may become increasingly combative, irritable, or antagonistic. Customers may also display nonverbal indicators of increased emotional reactivity, such as clenched fists, flushed cheeks, or quick breathing. Service providers need to be aware of these developments and react in a composed, professional, and patient manner. Service providers can assist in de-escalating tension and preventing disagreements from getting worse by maintaining their composure and empathy.

A rise in the complexity or intensity of the customer's expectations or requests may also be a sign of an escalation. Customers may increase their demands as their frustrations grow in an effort to take charge or find a solution to their problems. Service providers need to carefully evaluate the circumstances and realistically manage the expectations of their clients. Service providers can avoid escalation and concentrate on coming up with solutions that satisfy both parties by establishing limits and efficiently managing client expectations.

Customers occasionally use threats or violent behaviour to get what they want—a resolution to their complaints or to apply pressure. Threats of lawsuits, unfavourable reviews, or public humiliation can increase hostilities and make it more difficult for customer care representative to meet their needs. When faced with such behaviour, service providers should maintain their composure and avoid exacerbating the issue. Service providers might try to defuse tensions and offer positive solutions by being professional and making an effort to comprehend the underlying motives behind the customer's threats.

In conclusion, learning the art of customer service and navigating challenging conversations with ease depend on your ability to spot indicators of escalation. Service providers should take proactive measures to defuse tension and promote positive outcomes by paying close attention to emotional signs, complaints, conduct, and requests from their clients. Effective de-escalation strategies also help service providers maintain client connections, increase customer happiness, and maintain trust—all of which eventually improve the organization's performance and reputation. At the end of the day, providing excellent customer service is all about recognizing the warning signals of escalation, which benefits both customers and service providers.

Calming Strategies

Mastering the art of using calming techniques in customer service is not just a skill, but a key to handling difficult situations with composure, empathy, and professionalism. These techniques, also known as 'calming strategies ', are a diverse set of methods and strategies aimed at reducing stress, resolving disputes, and promoting constructive customer encounters. By equipping themselves with these techniques, service providers can navigate challenging circumstances, enhance client satisfaction, and uphold the integrity of the customer experience.

Active listening is a basic soothing technique that entails paying close attention to the client, empathically tapping into their problems, and validating their feelings. Active listening helps to reduce tension and foster a more encouraging and cooperative environment for problem-solving by showing the client that their issues are being heard and taken seriously. Helping to soothe the customer's emotions and start a productive conversation, service providers can do this by listening intently and reacting with empathy and understanding.

Empathy, a powerful soothing tactic, plays a crucial role in customer service encounters. It enables agents to connect with clients on a personal level, validating their feelings and experiences. True empathy goes beyond understanding the client's viewpoint; it involves showing genuine care and sympathy for their circumstances. By demonstrating empathy, service providers can help customers feel less frustrated, angry, or distressed, thereby building rapport and trust and facilitating the resolution of the situation at hand.

Using calming techniques in customer service contacts is not just about the techniques themselves, but about effective communication. This involves delivering messages in a courteous, firm, and clear manner. Service providers need to be confident and composed when speaking with clients, maintaining their composure and professionalism even in the face of difficult or aggressive conduct. By communicating effectively, service providers can help defuse tense situations, giving customers a sense of security and assurance.

Robust calming techniques like positivee language and framing can be used to diffuse tension and change the interaction's tone to one that is more constructive and upbeat. Service providers can show optimism about the conclusion of the encounter, highlight areas of agreement or potential solutions, and address the customer's worries by using positive language and phrasing. Service providers can assist in calming the customer's emotions and facilitating a more fruitful conversation by rephrasing the conversation in a positive perspective and concentrating on potential solutions rather than dwelling on the issue.

Using relaxation techniques to help service providers control their own stress and keep their cool during difficult situations is another useful soothing tactic. Methods like gradual muscle relaxation, deep breathing, and visualization can ease tension and anxiety while fostering calmness and clarity. Service workers can develop emotional self-regulation and resilience by implementing relaxation techniques into their daily routines. This will enable them to manage difficult circumstances with poise and comfort.

In customer service encounters, humour and lightheartedness can also be helpful calming techniques, relieving tension and fostering a more upbeat and comfortable environment. Service providers can gently diffuse uncomfortable situations, lighten the tone, and establish rapport with clients by using humour. Service providers can reduce tension and create a feeling of connection and camaraderie with customers by politely and appropriately incorporating humour into their interactions.

In conclusion, developing the skill of relaxing techniques is critical to handling challenging situations in the customer service industry with composure and professionalism. Service providers can effectively manage stress, defuse tensions, and promote positive outcomes in client encounters by using active listening, empathy, effective communication, positive language and framing, relaxing techniques, and humour. Calming techniques also contribute to the organization's success and reputation by maintaining relationships, enhancing the overall service experience, and strengthening trust. In the end, the key to providing outstanding customer service is the capacity to apply soothing techniques, which improves the lives of both consumers and service providers.

Redirecting Negative Energy

Redirecting negative energy is a crucial skill for service workers to have in the complex and dynamic world of customer service if they want to handle difficult contacts with professionalism, empathy, and grace. A variety of emotions, such as annoyance, rage, or customer unhappiness, might be signs of negative energy. Service providers can turn potentially explosive situations into chances for understanding, resolution, and positive outcomes by creating and putting into practice strategies to refocus negative energy. This will ultimately improve the overall customer experience and build long-term customer loyalty.

Engaging in active listening is an essential technique for deflecting negative energy. Being attentive to the client, recognizing their concerns, and expressing empathy are all parts of active listening. When service providers listen intently to customers' complaints or problems without criticizing or interjecting, they demonstrate empathy and respect. This eases tension and fosters a more positive atmosphere for productive conversation. Service providers can identify the root causes of a customer's unfavorable attitude and work toward mutually agreeable remedies by actively listening to them.

When it comes to rerouting negative energy in client contacts, empathy is a highly effective strategy. In order to be truly empathic, one must not only comprehend the viewpoint of the client but also show sincere care and sympathy for their circumstances. Service providers can help to defuse tension and establish rapport by showing empathy for the annoyances or worries of their clients. This promotes a sense of trust and understanding. Service providers can validate consumers' feelings, recognize their fears, and cooperate in resolving the situation at hand by responding with empathy.

Redirecting negative energy and turning challenging situations into chances for constructive participation requires effective communication skills. In spite of challenging client behavior, service personnel must communicate with clarity, empathy, and professionalism while keeping a cool head. Service providers can assist in reducing stress and refocusing the debate on constructive ideas by politely and assertively handling negative energy. Service providers can comfort clients, address their worries, and ultimately address the underlying problems causing their negative feelings by communicating effectively with them.

Framing the discourse in a positive way is another helpful tactic for deflecting negative energy. Customer service representatives are able to listen to their worries and irritations and point out advantages or possible solutions. Service providers can change the customer's viewpoint and promote a more positive discussion by rephrasing the conversation to centre on chances for resolution or improvement. Service providers can empower clients to feel heard, respected, and empowered to work toward a mutually satisfying outcome by using positive framing. Setting limits and properly handling client expectations are further strategies for deflecting negative energy.

In addition to controlling client expectations regarding the extent and timeliness of resolution, service providers need to set clear limits regarding acceptable behaviour and communication standards. Service providers can assist in reducing annoyance and halting the spread of bad vibes by communicating clearly and setting reasonable expectations. Even under challenging circumstances, service personnel may cultivate a sense of trust and confidence in the service experience by proactively managing expectations.

In conclusion, developing the skill of deflecting negative energy is critical to handling challenging situations in the customer service industry with composure and professionalism. Through the skilful redirection of negative energy, service professionals can preserve trust, strengthen relationships, and enhance the overall service experience, ultimately contributing to the success and reputation of the organization. Service professionals can transform negative interactions into opportunities for understanding, resolution, and positive outcomes by practising active listening, demonstrating empathy, communicating effectively, reframing conversations positively, and managing expectations. Refocusing negative energy to better the lives of both consumers and service providers is ultimately the key to providing exceptional customer service.

CHAPTER V

Problem-Solving Skills

Analyzing Issues and Identifying Solutions

To effectively negotiate difficult situations with grace, empathy, and proficiency in the complex world of customer service, service professionals must master the art of problem analysis and solution identification. An essential talent for guaranteeing successful outcomes and improving the entire customer experience is the capacity to assess problems and come up with acceptable solutions. Customer service encounters can entail complex topics, various views, and varying degrees of urgency. Professionals in the service industry may effectively handle client complaints, resolve disagreements, and cultivate enduring customer pleasure and loyalty by refining and enhancing their analytical and problem-solving abilities.

The capacity to actively listen to consumers' concerns and pinpoint the root causes of their discontent is a crucial part of problem-solving in customer service encounters. In order to engage in active listening, one must focus entirely on the client, pay attention to both verbal and nonverbal signs, and acknowledge their feelings and viewpoints with empathy. Careful listening and empathy-based listening help service providers understand the underlying causes of customer problems and develop focused, workable solutions that fully attend to customers' demands and concerns.

In customer service encounters, empathy is a fundamental component of practical issue analysis and solution discovery. In order to be truly empathic, one must not only comprehend the viewpoint of the client but also show sincere care and sympathy for their circumstances. Service providers can build rapport and trust with clients by being understanding of their needs, frustrations, and difficulties. This encourages candid communication and teamwork. Service providers can validate clients' feelings, reassure them that their issues are being taken seriously, and collaborate with them to discover mutually satisfying solutions by responding with empathy.

In customer service encounters, having practical communication skills is essential for assessing problems and coming up with solutions. In order to accurately and successfully communicate with clients and other pertinent stakeholders, service professionals need to speak with clarity, professionalism, and aggressiveness. By facilitating clear and concise communication between all parties involved, service providers can expedite the settlement process and minimize misunderstandings and miscommunications.

In customer service contacts, critical thinking abilities are essential for deciphering complicated problems and coming up with creative solutions. Service providers need to be able to look at things objectively, spot patterns or trends, and foresee any difficulties down the road. Service professionals may evaluate the practicality of different solutions, balance the benefits and drawbacks, and make well-informed decisions that support both corporate goals and the demands of consumers by using critical thinking abilities. Service experts are able to create solutions that are workable, long-lasting, and customized to the particulars of each client contact by using strategic research and careful thinking.

Practical issue analysis and solution identification in customer service encounters require cooperation and teamwork. In order to effectively utilize their combined skills and resources when solving problems, service professionals need to be able to work cooperatively with supervisors, coworkers, and other stakeholders. In order to solve customer problems and enhance the overall service experience, service professionals can leverage a variety of viewpoints, come up with innovative ideas, and put best practices into action by cultivating a culture of collaboration and information sharing inside the company.

Analyzing problems and finding solutions in customer service encounters requires constant learning and progress. In order to continuously improve their analytical and problem-solving abilities, service professionals need to be dedicated to continuous self-reflection, feedback, and professional growth. Service providers can enhance their methods for problem analysis and solution identification and learn a great deal about areas for improvement by asking for and receiving feedback from customers, coworkers, and supervisors. In addition, taking part in workshops, training sessions, and other educational opportunities can provide service professionals with fresh insights, tools, and methods to improve their problem-solving skills and continuously offer outstanding customer service.

In conclusion, developing the skills of problem-solving and analysis is critical to handling challenging situations in the customer service industry with composure and professionalism. Through attentive listening, empathetic communication, critical thinking, teamwork, and a commitment to ongoing improvement, service providers can skillfully handle client complaints, settle disputes, and improve the customer experience in general. In the end, the key to providing excellent customer service is having the analytical and problem-solving skills that benefit both customers and service providers.

Collaborative Problem-Solving with Customers

In order to effectively navigate difficult situations and promote positive outcomes, service professionals must learn the art of collaborative problem-solving with consumers. Customer service interactions can involve complicated problems and a range of viewpoints, necessitating a cooperative strategy that enables service providers and clients to cooperate in search of win-win solutions. Service providers can ensure that problems are resolved effectively and sympathetically while also strengthening client connections by adopting collaborative problem-solving approaches.

Active listening is the cornerstone of cooperative problem-solving with clients. Customer demands, complaints, and concerns must be actively listened to by service providers in order to show empathy and understanding. Service providers can find potential solutions that entirely meet customers' needs and gain a great deal of insight into the root causes of issues by providing consumers with the chance to fully express their ideas and experiences. Active listening helps to build a foundation of mutual respect, trust, and cooperation between clients and service providers.

In collaborative problem-solving with consumers, empathy acts as a compass, allowing service providers to comprehend and relate to consumers' feelings, viewpoints, and experiences. Customers are reassured by empathetic responses that their issues are acknowledged and cared for, which promotes an atmosphere that is conducive to candid dialogue and teamwork. Service providers can establish rapport, strengthen trust, and foster a feeling of shared purpose in resolving the issue at hand by acknowledging and validating clients' feelings. By engaging with empathy, service providers can build trusting relationships with clients and influence favorable outcomes in challenging situations.

In order to support cooperative problem-solving with clients, service providers must be able to communicate effectively in order to deliver information, concepts, and solutions. Service providers need to communicate in a transparent, professional, and clear manner to make sure that everyone is on the same page. Service providers can promote understanding and alignment, which will facilitate decision-making and collaboration, by effectively communicating their ideas and points of view. Customers that receive effective communication feel more confident, trusted, and empowered to actively contribute to problem-solving initiatives.

A proactive and solution-focused mindset is necessary for collaborative problem-solving with consumers. This approach enables service professionals to recognize chances for resolution and swiftly address customers' demands. When dealing with customer concerns, service personnel should adopt a problem-solving mindset, attempting to identify the underlying reasons of the issue and coming up with original solutions that satisfy clients' requirements and expectations. Service providers can use their knowledge and experience to create solutions that are workable, long-lasting, and customized to the particulars of each client encounter by actively including clients in the problem-solving process.

Being open to considering many viewpoints and ideas is another essential component of cooperative problem-solving with clients. Service providers need to be open-minded and responsive to client feedback, realizing that there might be several legitimate points of view and possible solutions to the problem at hand. Service professionals can leverage the collective wisdom and creativity of both customers and service providers by embracing diversity of thought and fostering an inclusive problem-solving environment. This approach can broaden the range of potential solutions and increase the likelihood of reaching a mutually satisfactory resolution.

Establishing clear expectations and encouraging accountability for execution and follow-through are other aspects of collaborative problem-solving with clients. Service providers must have an open and honest discussion with customers about the procedures necessary to resolve the issue as well as the roles and responsibilities of all parties involved. Service providers can guarantee that consumers are kept informed and involved throughout the process and that progress is made towards resolution by establishing reasonable deadlines, deliverables, and milestones. Service providers also need to be sure that solutions are implemented successfully and show that they are committed to customer satisfaction by actively following up on commitments made.

In order to effectively solve problems together with customers, service professionals must engage in continuous learning and improvement. This allows them to grow as professionals and increase their knowledge, abilities, and effectiveness over time. In order to learn from both achievements and setbacks in client encounters, service professionals must be dedicated to continual self-reflection, feedback, and professional growth. Service providers can enhance their collaborative problem-solving techniques and identify areas for development by soliciting feedback from supervisors, coworkers, and consumers. In addition, taking part in workshops, training sessions, and other educational opportunities can provide service professionals with fresh insights, tools, and methods to improve their problem-solving skills and continuously provide outstanding customer service.

To sum up, developing the skill of cooperative problem-solving with clients is crucial to handling challenging situations in the customer service industry with composure and professionalism. Service professionals can establish trust, improve communication, and ultimately fortify customer relationships by adopting active listening, empathy, effective problem-solving, proactive problem-solving, openness to alternative perspectives, accountability, and continuous improvement. They can also ensure that issues are resolved with efficiency and empathy. The secret to providing outstanding customer service is ultimately effective customer collaboration, which improves the lives of both consumers and service providers.

Turning Challenges into Opportunities

The capacity to convert obstacles into opportunities is a distinguishing feature of outstanding customer service. Customer complaints, miscommunications, or other challenging contacts offer service providers a chance to show their adaptability, sensitivity, and problem-solving skills. Service providers who are skilled at transforming obstacles into opportunities can not only handle challenging situations with ease but also develop rapport, promote trust, and improve the client experience in general.

Developing a proactive, solution-focused mentality is essential to converting obstacles into opportunities. Service workers perceive challenging interactions as chances for learning, development, and progress rather than as roadblocks or disappointments. Reframing difficulties as chances to show professionalism, competence, and empathy allows service providers to change their viewpoint and take advantage of the circumstance to improve customer relations and produce favourable results.

Empathy is the key to turning challenges into opportunities during customer service interactions. Empathy is the capacity to comprehend and establish a connection with the ideas, emotions, and experiences of clients—even in the midst of challenging or divisive circumstances. Serving customers with empathy for their worries, annoyances, and demands helps service providers build rapport, encourage candid conversation, and create a positive atmosphere for problem-solving. Service providers can turn difficult contacts into chances to strengthen bonds, establish rapport, and raise client satisfaction by engaging with empathy.

Service providers need to be able to communicate effectively in order to turn obstacles into opportunities and to deliver messages in a courteous, firm, and transparent manner. Service providers need to be confident and relaxed when speaking with clients, remaining collected even when faced with brutal conduct or conflicts. Service providers can improve understanding, reduce conflict, and foster trust with clients by communicating their views succinctly and precisely. This promotes a more favourable climate for cooperative problem-solving.

It also takes a proactive, solution-focused attitude to problem-solving to turn obstacles into possibilities. Service providers must be able to pinpoint the root reasons for client complaints, foresee future roadblocks or difficulties, and develop innovative solutions that fully attend to clients' needs. Service providers can show their dedication to client pleasure and promote successful outcomes in challenging interactions by acting proactively to resolve customer concerns and reduce potential hazards.

Adopting a growth mentality, which sees obstacles as chances for growth, development, and progress, is another essential component of transforming obstacles into opportunities. Service providers need to be receptive to criticism, eager to think back on their experiences, and dedicated to lifelong learning and development. Service providers can use challenging interactions as chances to improve their abilities, broaden their knowledge base, and provide better customer service by adopting a growth attitude.

In order to transform obstacles into opportunities in customer service encounters, cooperation and teamwork are essential. In order to effectively utilize the collective experience and resources in problem-solving endeavours, service professionals need to be able to cooperate with their peers, managers, and other relevant parties. In order to solve customer problems and improve the overall service experience, service professionals can use best practices, generate innovative ideas, and draw on a variety of viewpoints by cultivating a culture of collaboration and knowledge sharing inside the company.

Taking advantage of the chance to go above and beyond for customers and provide unforgettable experiences is another way to transform obstacles into opportunities. Service providers must be able to recognize chances to go above and beyond in order to meet customers' demands, solve their issues, and offer customized solutions. Service personnel who demonstrate flexibility, creativity, and a willingness to go above and beyond may turn challenging interactions into opportunities to satisfy customers, build loyalty, and differentiate their business from competitors.

In conclusion, developing the skill of transforming obstacles into opportunities is critical to handling challenging situations in the customer service industry with composure and professionalism. Support staff can turn complex interactions into chances for development, learning, and progress by taking a proactive approach, showing empathy, communicating clearly, accepting growth, encouraging teamwork, and grasping chances to go above and beyond for customers. At the end of the day, the key to providing excellent customer service is the capacity to transform obstacles into opportunities which benefit both customers and service providers.

CHAPTER VI

Setting Boundaries and Assertiveness

Establishing Clear Expectations

Setting clear expectations is a fundamental requirement in the ever-changing world of customer service if one is to navigate difficult conversations with grace, empathy, and professionalism. For both service providers and clients, well-defined expectations work as a road map that directs their interactions, resolves possible disputes, and eventually assures success. Service providers may build trust, improve communication, and provide outstanding client experiences that surpass expectations even in the most trying circumstances by being experts at setting clear expectations.

Proactive communication is a critical component in setting clear expectations. It is crucial for service providers to stay in constant communication with their clients, providing them with clear and accurate information about the products, services, and procedures that they are offering. Service providers can help to avoid misunderstandings, control client impressions, and foster confidence in the service experience by being explicit and upfront about their expectations from the start. In order to achieve mutually satisfying results, proactive communication fosters a collaborative and problem-solving atmosphere that benefits both customers and service providers.

When it comes to setting clear expectations in customer service conversations, empathy is essential. The ability to understand and connect with the needs, emotions, and perspectives of clients—even in the face of challenging or contentious situations—is known as empathy.

Service providers that demonstrate empathy for their clients' concerns, annoyances, and preferences can establish rapport and earn their trust. This will encourage open communication and create a welcoming environment where clear expectations can be set. By means of compassionate interaction, customer service representatives are able to anticipate their clients' requirements, attend to their worries, and guarantee that the services they receive meet or exceed their expectations.

Customer service representatives must be proficient communicators in order to establish clear expectations and provide information in a firm, polite, and open way. It is imperative for service providers to communicate with clients in a clear, professional, and transparent manner, making sure they comprehend the terms, conditions, and limitations of the goods or services they are providing. Service personnel can avoid misconceptions, control customer impressions, and reduce the likelihood of problems or disagreements by communicating expectations succinctly and precisely. Good communication gives consumers the confidence and trust they need to take charge of their experiences and make educated decisions.

Setting reasonable deadlines and objectives for resolving client complaints or issues is another aspect of clearly defining expectations. In order to ensure that customers know exactly what to anticipate and when to expect it, service personnel must manage customers' expectations regarding the extent, complexity, and timeliness of the resolution process. In order to control clients' perceptions and avoid frustrations or disappointments, service personnel should set realistic expectations and communicate openly and honestly with them throughout the service journey.

Setting limits and applying rules or regulations consistently are essential components of creating clear expectations. It is imperative for service professionals to proficiently convey and implement corporate policies, guidelines, and standards to clients, guaranteeing that they comprehend the terms of participation and the repercussions of non-adherence. Service providers can uphold professionalism, order, and respect in client interactions by establishing clear guidelines and expectations for appropriate behaviour and communication standards. This fosters a constructive environment that is conducive to problem-solving and resolution.

Setting clear expectations for customer service encounters requires cooperation and coordination. Service providers need to work well with managers, coworkers, and other stakeholders to make sure that expectations are clear and consistent at all organizational levels. Through cultivating a collaborative environment and knowledge exchange, service providers can harness a range of viewpoints, capitalize on group proficiency, and apply optimal techniques for setting and overseeing unambiguous expectations with clients. Working together guarantees accountability, consistency, and openness in customer contacts, which improves the overall quality of service and produces favourable results.

Setting clear expectations for customer service encounters is a technique that requires constant learning and growth. Service providers need to be dedicated to continuous self-evaluation, constructive criticism, and professional development. They should look for ways to improve their communication abilities, broaden their knowledge, and become more adept at establishing and upholding customer expectations. Service providers may enhance their methods of expectation management and learn a lot about areas for improvement by asking for and receiving feedback from customers, coworkers, and supervisors. In addition, taking part in workshops, training sessions, and other educational opportunities can provide service professionals with fresh insights, methods, and resources to improve their communication efficacy and continuously provide outstanding client experiences.

In conclusion, developing the skill of setting clear expectations is critical to handling challenging situations in the customer service industry with professionalism and ease. Service professionals can build trust, improve communication, and ultimately provide exceptional customer experiences by taking a proactive approach to communication, exhibiting empathy, communicating effectively, setting reasonable goals and boundaries, encouraging collaboration, and embracing continuous improvement. In the end, the key to providing excellent customer service is being able to clearly define expectations, which benefits both customers and service providers.

Assertive Communication Techniques

Knowing how to communicate assertively is crucial for handling difficult situations in the customer service industry with grace, professionalism, and efficiency. Service providers can boldly and effectively communicate their requirements, opinions, and thoughts while respecting the rights and viewpoints of clients when they use assertive communication. Service providers may improve the client experience and build strong connections by developing the skill of assertive communication. This includes setting limits, controlling expectations, and resolving problems in a civil and helpful way.

When someone communicates assertively, they do it in a straightforward, courteous manner and avoid using manipulation, aggression, or passive-aggressive behaviour. Service providers need to be able to listen intently to consumers, validate their viewpoints, and boldly state their demands and boundaries while looking for solutions that work for both parties. Service providers should foster a collaborative and open communication atmosphere by finding a balance between assertiveness and empathy. This will enable them to manage difficult circumstances with poise and comfort.

Using "I" statements to assertively and non-confrontationally communicate needs, feelings, and thoughts is an essential component of forceful communication. "I" statements do not place blame or accusation on the other person; instead, they centre on the speaker's own experiences and perceptions. For instance, a service professional might say, "I feel frustrated when I don't feel heard," as opposed to, "You're not listening to me." Service providers can communicate assertively and show empathy and respect for the opinions of their clients by employing "I" phrases.

In customer service encounters, assertive communication also involves active listening. Before answering, customer service representatives should pay close attention to the issues raised by their clients, validate their feelings, and make a sincere effort to grasp their viewpoints completely. Service providers can foster an atmosphere that is conducive to open communication and problem-solving by actively listening to others and exhibiting empathy and understanding. This will enable them to manage difficult circumstances with poise and comfort. In customer service encounters, assertive communication requires the establishment and maintenance of boundaries. Service providers need to be able to respectfully and assertively discuss their boundaries with clients while also being transparent about their expectations and standards. Service providers may avoid misunderstandings, manage expectations, and guarantee a courteous and pleasant service experience for all parties by setting boundaries around acceptable behaviour, communication standards, and service delivery procedures.

The capacity to respectfully and constructively express dissent or emphasize one's opinion is another aspect of assertive communication. Professionals in the service industry need to be able to confidently voice their thoughts, worries, or objections while still keeping an open mind to different perspectives and solutions. Service providers can promote open communication, inspire teamwork, and work toward mutually satisfying resolutions to client difficulties or conflicts by respectfully and assertively voicing disagreement.

In customer service encounters, forceful communication and conflict resolution are essential. In addition to advocating for their own needs and viewpoints, service professionals must be able to handle conflicts and disagreements in an aggressive and productive manner by trying to understand the underlying concerns and interests of all parties. Service professionals can negotiate disagreements with confidence, professionalism, and empathy by employing assertive communication tactics, including "I" statements, active listening, and boundary-setting. This will ultimately encourage positive results and enhance customer relationships.

The capacity to assertively negotiate and stand up for one's wants and interests in client contacts is another aspect of forceful communication. Service providers need to be able to confidently negotiate arrangements, concessions, or solutions that satisfy clients as well as their own demands. Service workers can improve the entire customer experience and build strong relationships by assertively and confidently advocating for their interests and making sure that their issues are addressed and that customers' demands are met.

In summary, developing assertive communication skills is critical to handling challenging situations in the customer service industry with poise and professionalism. Service providers can create clear communication, manage expectations, and settle disputes in a courteous and productive way by taking a balanced approach that incorporates assertiveness with empathy, active listening, boundary-setting, conflict resolution, negotiation, and advocacy skills. At the end of the day, the key to providing outstanding customer service is aggressive communication, which improves the lives of both clients and service providers.

Handling Boundary Violations

In order to manage challenging conversations with grace, empathy, and professionalism, customer service workers need to be adept at resolving boundary violations. Customers may transgress defined limitations, behave inappropriately, or disregard the rights and boundaries of service providers in order to constitute boundary violations. Service professionals who are skilled at handling boundary violations will be able to confidently set boundaries, effectively manage expectations, and uphold a respectful and safe environment for both themselves and their clients, ultimately improving the clientele's overall experience and cultivating positive relationships.

Recognizing and quickly identifying boundary violations is a basic component in handling them. Service providers need to be on the lookout for warning indications of boundary violations, such as offensive language, slights directed at them personally, or physical aggressiveness. Service providers can avoid the situation from getting worse by proactively addressing boundary violations and preventing them from getting worse.

Effectively managing boundary infractions relies heavily on assertive communication. Service providers need to be able to politely and confidently set boundaries and let clients know exactly what they expect from them. Service providers may voice their concerns in an aggressive manner while still exhibiting empathy and understanding for the viewpoints of their clients by employing assertive communication strategies, including "I" statements, active listening, and setting boundaries.

In customer service engagements, handling boundary infractions requires the establishment and maintenance of boundaries. In order to ensure that clients understand and respect these constraints, service professionals must set clear boundaries about acceptable behaviour, communication standards, and service delivery procedures. Service providers may avoid misunderstandings, control expectations, and create a polite and safe environment for both themselves and their clients by proactively establishing limits and regularly enforcing them.

In order to properly handle boundary violations in customer service interactions, conflict resolution skills are essential. In addition to advocating for their own needs and viewpoints, service professionals must be able to handle conflicts and disagreements in an aggressive and productive manner by trying to understand the underlying concerns and interests of all parties. Service workers can handle boundary violations with confidence, professionalism, and empathy by employing assertive communication strategies, active listening, and problem-solving abilities. This will ultimately lead to positive outcomes and build client relationships.

In order to respond to boundary infractions with tact and compassion, empathy is essential. Service providers need to be sensitive to and sympathetic to the feelings, viewpoints, and experiences of their clients, even in difficult or divisive circumstances. Serving customers with empathy allows service providers to establish rapport, diffuse conflict, and foster an atmosphere that is conducive to candid conversation and problem-solving.

Maintaining responsibility and successfully enforcing limits depend on clearly defining the consequences for boundary infractions. In order to guarantee that clients are aware of the repercussions of their actions, service providers need to convey and uphold organizational policies, norms, and standards in a consistent manner. Service providers can manage expectations, prevent inappropriate behavior, and uphold decorum and order in client interactions by clearly outlining expectations and the repercussions for crossing them.

Service providers must take care of themselves in order to stay resilient and in good health when dealing with boundary infractions. Because managing challenging relationships can be emotionally taxing and unpleasant, service providers need to put self-care first and ask for help when they need it. Service workers can refuel and restore their energy by engaging in self-care practices like mindfulness, relaxing, and asking for help from coworkers or superiors. This will allow them to handle difficult situations with poise and professionalism.

To sum up, managing boundary violations is an essential ability that service providers need to grasp in order to handle challenging situations in the customer service industry with assurance, professionalism, and empathy. Service professionals can confidently assert their boundaries, manage expectations, and uphold a safe and respectful environment for themselves and their clients by identifying boundary violations promptly, communicating assertively, setting and maintaining boundaries consistently, managing conflicts, demonstrating empathy, establishing clear consequences, and placing a high priority on self-care. In the end, the key to providing excellent customer service is the capacity to manage boundary transgressions with grace and professionalism, which benefits both clients and service providers.

CHAPTER VII

Handling Difficult Interactions in Different Channels

Phone Communication

Phone contact is still a significant means of communication between clients and customer service representatives in the current customer service environment. Being able to communicate effectively over the phone is crucial for handling challenging situations with grace, empathy, and professionalism. The inability to rely on visual clues and the possibility of misinterpretation due to variations in tone or intonation make phone encounters particularly difficult. Service workers may effectively manage difficult conversations, address customer complaints, and generate positive results that improve the entire customer experience by learning and improving their phone communication skills.

Active listening is a vital component of phone communication. When consumers ask questions, express concerns, or provide comments, service providers need to pay close attention to their tone of voice, word choice, and nonverbal indications. Service providers can show empathy, validate clients' feelings, and learn important information about their wants and preferences by actively listening to them. Establishing a rapport with consumers over the phone, responding to customer inquiries, and resolving difficulties quickly are all made possible by service workers who actively listen.

The foundation of phone communication is empathy, which allows agents to comprehend and relate to the feelings, viewpoints, and experiences of their clients. Customers feel more trusted and connected when they receive empathetic responses, which show them that their worries are understood and valued. Service providers can foster an atmosphere of open communication and compassion by showing empathy for the problems or difficulties that customers have. This allows them to respond to client issues in a kind and considerate manner.

Service providers need to be able to communicate effectively in order to handle challenging phone conversations and provide information in a clear, succinct, and confident manner. It is imperative for service workers to interact with consumers in a clear, professional, and empathetic manner to ensure that messages are understood and applied correctly. Service providers may avoid misunderstandings, control expectations, and confidently and professionally handle client complaints by communicating their ideas and opinions in a clear and forceful manner.

Maintaining a customer's attention and engagement over the phone requires active participation. For consumers' needs and concerns to be met, service providers must actively engage them in discussion, ask open-ended questions, and request feedback. Through proactive interaction with clients, service providers can show that they are dedicated to meeting their needs, spot areas where their services may be improved, and create an exceptional customer experience.

Effective phone conversation requires the ability to solve problems, which helps customer care representatives respond to inquiries and handle issues quickly and effectively. In order to satisfy the needs of their customers, service providers must be able to identify the root causes of issues brought up by customers, develop novel solutions, and implement such solutions.

Service professionals use their problem-solving skills to manage challenging circumstances with ease, attend to client concerns, and ensure effective outcomes that enhance the customer experience.

In order to effectively handle difficult phone contacts and resolve client complaints and disputes, service personnel need to possess conflict resolution abilities. Service providers need to be able to resolve disputes amicably and assertively, looking to understand the underlying concerns and goals of each side. Service providers can resolve disagreements professionally and empathetically by employing active listening, empathy, and problem-solving techniques. This will ultimately lead to positive outcomes and improve customer relationships.

In order to prioritize client inquiries, control call traffic, and immediately attend to customer demands, service personnel must possess strong time management abilities. Effective time management is essential for service providers to make sure they set aside enough time and resources to handle client issues and deliver high-quality service. Service providers may avoid delays, reduce wait times, and guarantee that clients receive prompt phone support and help by effectively managing their time.

Effective phone communication requires adaptability because it allows customer care representatives to modify their strategy and style of communication to accommodate a wide range of clientele's wants and preferences. Service providers need to be flexible in their communication to suit various cultural backgrounds, communication styles, and preferences. Service providers can establish connection, promote comprehension, and guarantee efficient phone conversation with clients by exhibiting flexibility and adaptability.

The art of phone communication requires constant learning and progress, which helps service providers become more proficient over time by honing their abilities, expanding their knowledge, and increasing their efficacy. Apart from actively pursuing opportunities to gain insights from both successes and failures in phone conversations, customer service representatives must be committed to ongoing self-evaluation, constructive criticism, and career advancement. Service providers who solicit feedback from consumers, coworkers, and supervisors can enhance their phone communication techniques and pinpoint areas that require improvement.

To sum up, becoming proficient in phone conversation is crucial to handling challenging situations in the customer service industry with poise and professionalism. Service professionals can effectively manage challenging interactions, address customer concerns, and foster positive outcomes that enhance the overall customer experience by developing and honing their skills in active listening, empathy, effective communication, problem-solving, conflict resolution, time management, adaptability, and continuous improvement. In the end, the key to providing excellent customer service is having strong phone communication skills, which improve the lives of both clients and service providers.

Email Correspondence

Email contact has become an essential part of customer service interactions in the current digital era. Service providers must become adept at email communication in order to handle challenging situations with professionalism, sensitivity, and grace. Email exchanges pose particular difficulties because there are no visual or audio clues available, meaning that tone or intent could be misunderstood, and clear and succinct communication is essential. Service providers can handle difficult situations, resolve client complaints, and promote favourable results that improve the customer experience by honing their email communication skills.

An essential component of efficient email communication is active listening. Customer emails must be thoroughly read and comprehended by service providers, who should pay close attention to the subtleties of language, tone, and emotion. Service providers can show empathy, confirm customers' experiences, and learn important information about their wants and preferences by carefully listening to their complaints and feedback. In order to appropriately respond to client inquiries and address concerns with care and attention to detail, service professionals must first engage in meaningful discourse and problem-solving. This is made possible through active listening.

The foundation of email communication is empathy, which allows customer care representatives to comprehend and relate to the feelings, viewpoints, and experiences of their clients. Customers are shown that their worries are respected and acknowledged when they receive empathetic responses, which builds rapport and trust. Service providers can foster an atmosphere of open communication and compassion by showing empathy for the problems or difficulties that customers have. This allows them to respond to client issues in a kind and considerate manner.

Effective email communication requires precision and succinctness, especially when handling challenging situations. Service providers need to communicate information in a clear, concise, and professional manner that leaves no room for confusion and is easy to understand. Service providers should minimize misconceptions and misinterpretations by using plain language, staying away from jargon and technical phrases, and rationally structuring information. This promotes effective communication and improves the customer experience in general.

Maintaining customer satisfaction and confidence requires timely responses to communications. Customer emails must be immediately acknowledged by service providers, and questions or concerns must be addressed in a timely manner. Service providers can communicate a feeling of urgency and dedication to customer satisfaction by being prompt and sensitive to their demands. This helps to establish trust and develop favourable consumer perceptions.

Effective email communication requires the ability to solve problems since it helps customer service representatives to respond to inquiries and handle problems quickly. To satisfy customers' requirements and expectations, service professionals need to be able to determine the underlying reasons for customer problems, effectively assess information, and provide suitable solutions. Service experts can handle difficult situations with ease, respond quickly to customer problems, and guarantee successful outcomes that improve the customer experience by utilizing their problem-solving abilities.

In order to effectively handle challenging email encounters and resolve client complaints or disputes, service workers need to possess conflict resolution abilities. Service providers need to be able to resolve disputes amicably and assertively, looking to understand the underlying concerns and goals of each side. Service providers can resolve disagreements professionally and empathetically by employing active listening, empathy, and problem-solving techniques. This will ultimately lead to positive outcomes and improve customer relationships. Email correspondence must always be professional since it represents the company and its reputation. In all email correspondence, service providers need to keep a professional tone and manner; they should refrain from using any language or acting in a way that could be interpreted as disrespectful or careless. Service personnel can communicate expertise, dependability, and trustworthiness to clients by following organizational policies and guidelines, using good syntax and punctuation, and editing emails for accuracy and clarity.

Effective email communication requires adaptability since it allows service providers to modify their strategy and communication style to suit the demands and tastes of a wide range of clients. Service providers need to be flexible with their tone, vocabulary, and formality to suit various cultural backgrounds, communication preferences, and styles. Service providers can establish connections, promote comprehension, and guarantee efficient email contact with clients by exhibiting flexibility and adaptability.

Becoming proficient in email communication requires constant learning and progress, which helps service providers become more knowledgeable, skilled, and productive over time. Service providers need to be dedicated to continuous self-evaluation, constructive criticism, and professional growth. They should look for chances to take lessons from both positive and negative email exchanges. Service providers may improve their email communication strategies and identify areas for development by getting feedback from customers, coworkers, and supervisors.

To sum up, becoming proficient in email communication is crucial for handling challenging situations in the customer service industry with poise and professionalism. Service professionals can effectively manage challenging interactions, address customer concerns, and foster positive outcomes that enhance the overall service experience by developing and honing their skills in active listening, empathy, clarity, responsiveness, problem-solving, conflict resolution, professionalism, adaptability, and continuous improvement. Effective email communication is ultimately the foundation of providing outstanding customer service, which improves the lives of both clients and service providers.

Live Chat Support

Live chat support has become an essential tool for customer service interactions in the fast-paced digital world. It provides clients with rapid assistance and real-time solutions to their questions and issues. Service providers must become experts at live chat support if they want to handle difficult situations with grace, empathy, and professionalism. Due to text-based communication, live chat engagements pose specific issues, such as prompt response requirements, the lack of visual and audio signals, and the possibility of misinterpretation. Service providers may handle challenging encounters, resolve customer problems, and promote positive outcomes that improve the entire customer experience by honing their live chat support skills.

A key component of providing excellent live chat help is active listening. Service providers must carefully read and understand customer messages and must pay close attention to the subtleties of language, tone, and emotion. Service providers can show empathy, confirm customers' experiences, and learn important information about their wants and preferences by carefully listening to their complaints and feedback. The foundation of meaningful conversation and problem-solving is active listening, which helps customer service representatives answer questions from customers and handle situations with precision and compassion.

In order for live chat support agents to comprehend and relate to consumers' feelings, viewpoints, and experiences, empathy is a critical component. Customers are shown that their worries are respected and acknowledged when they receive empathetic responses, which builds rapport and trust. Service providers can foster an atmosphere of open communication and compassion by showing empathy for the problems or difficulties that customers have. This allows them to respond to client issues in a kind and considerate manner.

Effective live chat conversation requires precision and succinctness, especially when handling challenging situations. Service providers need to communicate information in a clear, concise, and professional manner that leaves no room for confusion and is easy to understand. Service providers should minimize misconceptions and misinterpretations by using plain language, staying away from jargon and technical phrases, and rationally structuring information. This promotes effective communication and improves the customer experience in general.

It is essential to reply to messages from customers right away in order to keep their confidence and happiness. Customer questions and concerns must be swiftly acknowledged by service providers, who then have to respond quickly and give pertinent information or answers. Service providers can communicate a feeling of urgency and dedication to customer satisfaction by being prompt and sensitive to their demands. This helps to establish trust and develop favourable consumer perceptions.

Practical live chat assistance requires problem-solving abilities from service providers in order to handle client concerns and problems quickly and effectively. In order to satisfy customers' requirements and expectations, service professionals need to be able to determine the underlying reasons for customer problems, effectively assess information, and provide suitable solutions. Service experts can handle difficult situations with ease, respond quickly to customer problems, and guarantee successful outcomes that improve the customer experience by utilizing their problem-solving abilities.

In order to effectively handle challenging encounters in live chat support and resolve client complaints or disputes, service providers need to possess conflict resolution abilities. Service providers need to be able to resolve disputes amicably and assertively, looking to understand the underlying concerns and goals of each side. Service providers can resolve disagreements professionally and empathetically by employing active listening, empathy, and problem-solving techniques. This will ultimately lead to positive outcomes and improve customer relationships.

Since live chat helps represent the company and its brand, professionalism is essential. In all live chat conversations, customer service representatives should keep a professional tone and manner, refraining from using any language or acting in a way that could come across as disrespectful or careless. Service providers can project competence, dependability, and trustworthiness to clients by abiding by organizational norms and guidelines, utilizing good grammar and punctuation, and delivering accurate and pertinent information.

Since it enables agents to adjust their approach and communication style to suit the needs and preferences of a wide range of clients, flexibility is a prerequisite for providing adequate live chat service. Service providers need to be flexible with their tone, vocabulary, and formality to suit various cultural backgrounds, communication preferences, and styles. In live chat engagements, customer care representatives can establish rapport, promote comprehension, and guarantee efficient communication by exhibiting flexibility and adaptability.

Gaining proficiency in live chat support requires constant learning and improvement, which helps support staff members become more knowledgeable, skilled, and productive over time. In order to learn from both achievements and setbacks in live chat encounters, service professionals need to be dedicated to continuous self-reflection, feedback, and professional development. Service providers may improve their live chat support strategies and identify areas for improvement by getting feedback from customers, coworkers, and managers.

To sum up, becoming an expert in live chat support is crucial to handling challenging situations in the customer service industry with poise and professionalism. Service professionals can effectively manage challenging interactions, address customer concerns, and foster positive outcomes that enhance the overall service experience by developing and honing their skills in active listening, empathy, clarity, responsiveness, problem-solving, conflict resolution, professionalism, adaptability, and continuous improvement. Ultimately, having effective communication skills in live chat interactions is essential to provide exceptional customer support, which benefits both service providers and customers.

Social Media Engagement

Social media has developed into a potent tool for consumer connection and engagement in the digital age. Service providers must become experts at social media participation if they want to handle difficult situations with grace, empathy, and professionalism. Social media platforms have distinctive prospects for customer service, permitting instantaneous communication, public engagements, and the possibility of viral dissemination. They do, however, also bring particular difficulties, such as the requirement to control public opinion, respond to criticism, and preserve brand reputation. Service personnel may effectively manage challenging conversations, address customer concerns, and generate positive results that improve the entire customer experience by honing their social media engagement abilities.

One of the most critical components of successful social media participation is active listening. Service providers need to keep a close eye on social media platforms and respond to any messages, comments, or feedback from clients. Service providers can show empathy, confirm customers' experiences, and learn important information about their wants and preferences by carefully listening to their worries and thoughts. The foundation of meaningful conversation and problem-solving is active listening, which helps customer service representatives answer questions from customers and handle situations with precision and compassion.

When it comes to interacting with clients on social media, empathy is essential because it allows service providers to relate to and comprehend their feelings, viewpoints, and experiences. Customers are shown that their worries are respected and acknowledged when they receive empathetic responses, which builds rapport and trust. Service providers can foster an atmosphere of open communication and compassion by showing empathy for the problems or difficulties that customers have. This allows them to respond to client issues in a kind and considerate manner.

Effective social media involvement requires openness and clarity, especially when handling challenging situations. It is imperative for service providers to communicate in a clear, honest, and transparent manner, making sure that the message is unambiguous and easy to comprehend. Even under challenging circumstances, service providers can gain the credibility and trust of clients by giving accurate information and directly admitting faults.

Maintaining customer satisfaction and trust on social media requires quick responses to questions and feedback from customers. Customer comments and communications must be swiftly acknowledged by service personnel, who then have to respond quickly and provide pertinent information or solutions. Service providers can communicate a feeling of urgency and dedication to customer satisfaction by being prompt and sensitive to their demands. This helps to establish trust and develop favourable consumer perceptions.

Effective social media involvement requires problem-solving abilities, which let customer support representatives respond to queries and handle problems quickly and effectively. In order to satisfy customers' requirements and expectations, service professionals need to be able to determine the underlying reasons for customer problems, effectively assess information, and provide suitable solutions. Service experts can handle difficult situations with ease, respond quickly to customer problems, and guarantee successful outcomes that improve the customer experience by utilizing their problem-solving abilities.

In order for service providers to properly handle consumer complaints or conflicts on social media, they need to possess conflict resolution abilities. Service providers need to be able to resolve disputes amicably and assertively, looking to understand the underlying concerns and goals of each side. Service providers can resolve disagreements professionally and empathetically by employing active listening, empathy, and problem-solving techniques. This will ultimately lead to positive outcomes and improve customer relationships.

When using social media, professionalism is essential since it represents the company's reputation and image. In all social media contacts, service providers need to keep a professional tone and manner; they should refrain from using any language or acting in a way that could come across as rude or careless. Service providers can project competence, dependability, and trustworthiness to clients by abiding by organizational norms and guidelines, utilizing good grammar and punctuation, and delivering accurate and pertinent information.

Effective social media engagement requires adaptability since it allows service providers to modify their strategy and communication style to suit the demands and preferences of a wide range of clients. Service providers need to be flexible with their tone, vocabulary, and formality to suit various cultural backgrounds, communication preferences, and styles. Service providers can establish connections, promote understanding, and guarantee efficient contact with clients on social media platforms by exhibiting flexibility and adaptation.

Becoming proficient in social media engagement requires constant learning and progress, which helps service providers become more knowledgeable, skilled, and productive over time. In order to learn from both achievements and setbacks in social media interactions, service professionals need to be dedicated to continuous self-reflection, feedback, and professional development. Service providers can improve their methods to social media participation and identify areas for improvement by soliciting input from consumers, coworkers, and supervisors.

In conclusion, developing your social media engagement skills is crucial to handling challenging situations in the customer service industry with poise and professionalism. Service professionals can effectively manage challenging interactions, address customer concerns, and foster positive outcomes that enhance the overall service experience by developing and honing their skills in active listening, empathy, clarity, responsiveness, problem-solving, conflict resolution, professionalism, adaptability, and continuous improvement. After all, the secret to providing outstanding customer service—which benefits both clients and service providers—lies in knowing how to interact with others on social media.

CHAPTER VIII

Leveraging Technology and Tools

CRM Systems and Customer Data Management

Client relationship management (CRM) systems and efficient client data management have emerged as critical tools in the digital age, helping organizations to provide outstanding customer service. In order to handle challenging contacts with grace, empathy, and professionalism, service professionals must become experts at using CRM systems and effectively managing customer data. CRM systems provide valuable insights into the preferences, actions, and interactions of customers by centralizing and organizing customer data. Service providers can anticipate client demands, personalize contacts, and quickly handle difficulties by utilizing CRM systems and efficiently managing customer data. This improves the customer experience in general and builds strong customer connections.

Customer data, such as contact information, purchase history, preferences, and interactions, are centrally stored and managed by CRM systems. CRM systems provide service personnel with access to detailed customer profiles, which offer them a thorough understanding of each client and their connection with the company. Service providers can monitor client interactions through several channels, spot trends or patterns, and customize their approach to each customer's specific needs and preferences by using CRM systems successfully.

Ensuring the integrity, dependability, and security of customer information in CRM systems requires effective customer data management. Service providers need to make sure that client data is accurate, full, and consistent across all channels by following best practices for data entry, validation, and upkeep. Service providers can reduce errors, avoid duplication, and guarantee that they have access to trustworthy information when interacting with clients by keeping their customer data clean and accurate.

To effectively use CRM systems for customer service, data segmentation and analysis are essential. Customer data can be segmented by service providers according to a range of factors, including demographics, past purchases, and degree of interaction, in order to pinpoint target groups and tailor marketing tactics. Service providers can find actionable insights, spot upselling and cross-selling opportunities, and customize marketing campaigns and service offerings to cater to the unique requirements and preferences of various customer segments by examining customer data insights within CRM systems.

CRM systems with automation and workflow management features increase productivity and streamline customer service procedures. By utilizing CRM system functions, service workers can automate repetitive duties like email responses and appointment scheduling, freeing up time to concentrate on more intricate customer questions or difficulties. By employing automated capabilities, service providers can ensure precision, swiftness, and uniformity in their client communications, thereby enhancing customer satisfaction and boosting efficiency.

To maximize CRM systems' efficacy in customer service, integration with other company systems and applications is crucial. To centralize data and improve workflows, service providers can combine CRM systems with a range of platforms and tools, including email marketing software, helpdesk solutions, and social media monitoring tools. Service providers can track client interactions across different channels, access real-time information, and offer seamless, customized customer experiences by integrating CRM systems with other corporate systems.

When it comes to client data management and CRM systems, security and compliance are crucial factors. Strict security procedures and data protection laws must be followed by service providers in order to protect client information and guarantee privacy and confidentiality. By putting robust security measures in place—like encryption, access controls, and regular audits—service providers can lessen the chance of data breaches and maintain customers' trust in the way their business manages customer data.

To enable service personnel to use CRM systems efficiently and harness client data for the best possible service delivery, training and education are crucial. To guarantee that service personnel have the ability to use CRM systems with assurance and morality, organizations need to offer thorough training courses and other resources. Service professionals may continually provide consumers with outstanding service by investing in their professional development and continuing education. This will enable them to stay informed on developments in customer relationship management (CRM) and customer data management, including industry trends, best practices, and upcoming technologies.

Learning the art of CRM systems and customer data management in customer service requires constant innovation and refinement. In order to improve the customer experience, service personnel need to be proactive in getting input from peers and consumers, pinpointing areas that need work, and investigating novel approaches to use CRM systems and customer data. Service personnel can stay ahead of the curve, adjust to shifting client demands and preferences, and provide excellent service that goes above and beyond what customers expect by adopting a culture of innovation and constant learning.

In conclusion, negotiating challenging interactions in the field of customer service with ease and professionalism requires mastery of the use of CRM systems and the management of client data. In order to anticipate client demands, immediately handle issues, and cultivate positive connections that create customer loyalty and satisfaction, service personnel can use CRM systems to centralize customer information, customize interactions, expedite processes, and optimize workflows. Delivering outstanding customer service experiences that improve the lives of both consumers and service personnel ultimately comes down to the ability to leverage the power of CRM systems and customer data.

Automated Responses and Chatbots

Chatbots and automated responses have transformed customer service interactions in today's fast-paced digital environment by providing prompt support and practical solutions to customers' questions and issues. Service providers must become adept at using chatbots and automated responses if they want to handle challenging situations with professionalism, empathy, and grace. These automated solutions improve customer service overall, expedite procedures, and offer prompt support. They do, however, also bring with them particular difficulties, such as the requirement to strike a balance between automation and human touch, guarantee response accuracy, and continue to take a customized approach to consumer contacts. Service providers can effectively use chatbots and automated responses to handle challenging encounters, resolve customer problems, and promote favourable outcomes that increase customer satisfaction and loyalty by knowing their capabilities and limitations.

The capacity of chatbots and automated responses to offer clients prompt support at any time of day is one of its main advantages. With the help of these automated technologies, service providers may concentrate on more complicated client concerns by handling typical queries like FAQs and simple troubleshooting. Chatbots and computerised responses improve customer service accessibility and availability by providing prompt and effective responses. This guarantees that consumers receive timely support whenever they need it.

Even while chatbots and automated responses are quick and effective, they must be used carefully to avoid any potential problems. Making sure chatbots and automated responses are precise and pertinent to clients' questions is a frequent problem. Service providers need to carefully plan and develop chatbots and automated responses in order to comprehend and efficiently handle a variety of client inquiries. Service providers may keep their client interactions accurate and relevant by routinely reviewing and upgrading chatbots and automated responses in light of consumer feedback and changing needs.

Finding the ideal mix between automation and human interaction is another difficulty when using chatbots and automated responses. Although automated technologies are more efficient, they should maintain the empathy and personalization that consumers come to expect from face-to-face interactions. In order to simulate human-like communication, service providers must build chatbots and automated responses that incorporate sentiment analysis and natural language processing to comprehend better and address the emotions of their clients. Customer service representatives may guarantee that clients feel appreciated and understood even while working with technology by adding a human touch to automated interactions.

Service providers also need to be aware of the limitations of chatbots and automated responses when it comes to managing delicate or complicated client situations. Although these tools are pretty good at answering simple questions, they might need help to handle complex or emotionally charged encounters which call for human assistance. In order to guarantee that clients receive the individualized attention and assistance they require to address their concerns successfully, service providers must be ready to step in and escalate conversations to human agents when needed. Through the seamless integration of chatbots and automated responses with human support channels, service professionals can offer consumers a comprehensive and seamless service experience that caters to their varied demands.

Notwithstanding these difficulties, chatbots and automated responses present a wealth of chances for customer support representatives to optimize workflows, boost productivity, and elevate the customer experience in general. Service providers can benefit from these solutions by managing large amounts of questions, speeding up response times, and guaranteeing channel consistency in communication. Service providers can free up time to concentrate on other value-added activities, like developing connections with clients, seeing upselling and cross-selling opportunities, and offering individualized support that goes above and beyond for clients by strategically utilizing automation.

Moreover, chatbots and automated responses can be helpful to data gathering instruments that reveal information about the preferences, behavior, and problems of customers. Service providers can use data collected from automated interactions to spot patterns, streamline workflows, and adjust their strategy to suit changing client demands. Service providers may make well-informed decisions, promote continuous improvement in customer service operations, and provide exceptional experiences that increase customer happiness and loyalty by utilizing data analytics.

Finally, in order to handle challenging contacts in the field of customer service with professionalism and ease, it is imperative to become proficient in the use of chatbots and automated responses. Service providers can effectively use automation to improve the accessibility, effectiveness, and personalization of customer service interactions by being aware of the tool's capabilities and limitations. In order to guarantee that clients receive prompt support, tailored assistance, and, in the end, a satisfying service experience that encourages advocacy and loyalty, service professionals must strike the correct balance between automation and human touch. The secret to using chatbots and automated responses effectively is to blend technology with human empathy and connection to provide outstanding customer service that goes above and beyond what is expected.

Using Data Analytics for Customer Insights

Leveraging data analytics for customer insights has become critical for firms looking to provide outstanding customer service in today's data-driven environment. Service providers must become experts at leveraging data analytics to gain consumer insights in order to handle challenging situations with tact, empathy, and professionalism. With the help of data analytics, service providers may better understand client behaviour, preferences, and pain spots, which helps them predict demands, tailor interactions, and successfully handle problems. However, there are a number of obstacles to overcome when utilizing data analytics, such as problems with data quality, privacy issues, and the requirement for highly developed analytical abilities. Service workers can use data to handle challenging encounters, address customer problems, and promote positive outcomes that improve the entire service experience by knowing the possibilities and limitations of data analytics.

Gaining a thorough picture of customer behavior across several touchpoints is one of the main advantages of employing data analytics for customer insights. Data from a range of sources, including as customer contacts, transactions, and feedback, can tell service providers a lot about their customers' preferences, routines, and stages of the customer journey. With the use of these insights, customer service representatives may adjust their strategy to each individual's specific needs, anticipate their preferences, and provide individualized experiences that increase customer happiness and loyalty.

Despite the enormous potential that data analytics offer for gaining client insights, service providers still need help with issues with data quality and dependability. Making sure that data is accurate, comprehensive, and consistent is crucial to getting valuable insights from data analytics. To guarantee that the conclusions drawn from data analytics are trustworthy and applicable, service providers need to deal with problems, including data silos, redundant records, and out-of-date information. In order to improve decision-making and customer service outcomes, service professionals should boost the accuracy and reliability of their data analytics efforts by putting data quality management practices into place and investing in technologies for data cleansing and validation.

Upholding client privacy and data security presents another difficulty when employing data analytics for customer insights. When handling client data, service providers are subject to stringent privacy legislation and ethical standards that must be followed to protect sensitive information from misuse or unauthorized access. Service providers that implement robust data security measures, like encryption, access controls, and data anonymization strategies, can preserve consumer privacy and promote confidence in the way their company handles personal data. Furthermore, preserving openness and accountability in data analytics projects requires open communication with clients regarding data gathering and usage procedures. Service providers that implement robust data security measures, like encryption, access controls, and data anonymization strategies, can preserve consumer privacy and promote confidence in the way their company handles personal data. Furthermore, maintaining transparency and accountability in data analytics initiatives necessitates candid discussions about data collection and utilization practices with clients.

Furthermore, in order to properly extract valuable insights from data analytics, service personnel need to have advanced analytical skills and competencies. Proficiency in data manipulation, statistical analysis, and data visualization techniques is necessary when analyzing massive volumes of data. It is imperative for service professionals to possess the ability to comprehend intricate data sets, recognize patterns and trends, and derive practical insights that facilitate strategy formulation and decision-making. Service professionals can enable themselves to fully utilize data analytics for customer insights by investing in training and development programs that strengthen analytical skills. This will promote innovation and continual improvement in the provision of customer service.

The advantages of employing data analytics for customer insights are significant, notwithstanding these difficulties. Service providers can find chances for revenue development, service innovation, and process improvement with the use of data analytics. Service providers can see areas for service delivery improvement, such as faster response times, better resource allocation, and better product offerings, by studying customer data. Furthermore, data analytics can help guide focused marketing strategies, allowing service providers to segment their clientele according to their tastes and habits and create customized marketing campaigns that appeal to specific target markets.

Additionally, proactive problem-solving and issue resolution in customer support interactions can be facilitated by data analytics. Service providers can recognize reoccurring problems or pain areas and take proactive measures to address them before they worsen by examining past data and client feedback. Service providers are able to anticipate the wants and preferences of their customers through the use of predictive analytics techniques such as machine learning and predictive modeling. As a result, they are able to offer prompt help and tailored recommendations that improve the general client experience.

To sum up, if you want to navigate challenging customer service interactions with professionalism and ease, you must become an expert at applying data analytics for consumer insights. Service providers may efficiently use data to obtain actionable insights into the behaviour, preferences, and pain points of their customers by knowing the potential and constraints of data analytics. Service providers can fully utilize data analytics to spur innovation and continual improvement in customer service delivery by tackling issues with data quality, privacy, and analytical abilities. At the end of the day, providing outstanding customer service experiences that surpass expectations and promote enduring customer loyalty and advocacy ultimately comes down to the ability to leverage the power of data analytics.

CHAPTER IX

Team Collaboration and Support

Peer Support Networks

Peer support networks have become essential tools for customer service professionals who want to handle challenging situations in the field with professionalism and ease. These networks give peers going through comparable struggles and experiences the chance to work together, share expertise, and provide emotional support. Service providers must learn how to use peer support networks effectively if they hope to improve their abilities, obtain new perspectives, and develop resilience in handling complex client interactions. By participating in peer support networks, service providers can get access to a range of perspectives, learn from one another's experiences, and develop coping skills for difficult situations. This enhances the overall service experience and promotes a culture of ongoing learning and growth.

The chance for service providers to impart knowledge and experience to their peers is one of the main advantages of peer support networks. Service providers can share best practices, plans, and methods for handling challenging client interactions among themselves via peer support networks. Service providers can obtain critical insights into practical strategies for overcoming typical problems, like dealing with furious clients, handling complicated difficulties, or handling high-stress circumstances, by studying the experiences of others.

Peer support networks facilitate collaboration and group problem-solving, giving service professionals access to the collective knowledge of their peers, which helps them improve their own customer service skills and capacities.

Peer support networks also offer emotional support and companionship to professionals in the service industry who are coping with the stress and responsibilities of customer service positions. Engaging with colleagues who comprehend the distinct difficulties and strains associated with providing customer service can offer support, compassion, and affirmation to help service providers manage challenging exchanges with ease. Peer support networks promote a welcoming environment where service workers can share their problems, celebrate accomplishments, and seek counsel or advice from others who have been in similar situations. They also help members feel a feeling of connection and solidarity. Peer support networks improve the resilience and general well-being of service workers by providing emotional support and camaraderie, which helps them deal calmly and confidently with difficult situations.

Peer support networks also help service workers in customer service professions with ongoing education and professional growth. Service providers can obtain training, courses, and resources catered to their unique requirements and obstacles by engaging in peer support networks. Within these networks, peer-led talks, mentoring programs, and knowledge-sharing sessions allow service professionals to broaden their skill set, stay current with industry developments, and pick up new tools and methods for providing outstanding customer service. Customer service agents can become more adept at handling difficult situations and provide better experiences and outcomes for clients by investing resources in ongoing education and training.

Peer support networks provide chances for networking and career improvement for service workers, in addition to exchanging expertise and providing emotional support. By connecting with colleagues from various industries and backgrounds through these networks, service professionals can broaden their professional network and cultivate connections that may result in joint ventures or job prospects. Peer support networks offer venues for acknowledgement and visibility among the community of customer service providers, enabling service providers to highlight their accomplishments, experiences, and contributions to the industry. Service professionals can expand their employment opportunities, improve their professional reputation, and set themselves up for success in their customer service jobs by actively participating in peer support networks.

Even with the manifold advantages that peer support networks provide for service providers, there exist certain obstacles and factors to be mindful of while utilizing them. Making sure peer support networks are inclusive and diverse so that all participants feel respected and welcomed is one of the challenges. Service providers need to be aware of potential biases, preconceptions, and power dynamics in peer support groups and take proactive measures to establish inclusive environments where all participants are treated with respect and feel supported. Peer support networks can leverage the abilities and views of their members to drive innovation and excellence in customer service by promoting diversity and inclusivity.

In order to fully benefit from peer support networks, service professionals also need to participate in and contribute to these networks actively. It is insufficient for service professionals to belong to a peer support network merely; in order to foster a lively and cooperative community, they must share their experiences, connect meaningfully, and offer support to one another. Service professionals can benefit from the professional development, emotional support, and information sharing that peer support networks provide by devoting time and energy to them. This will ultimately increase their efficacy and resilience in handling challenging client interactions.

To sum up, in order for service providers to handle challenging situations in the customer service industry with poise and professionalism, they must become proficient in using peer support networks. Service providers can get information, emotional support, and professional development opportunities that improve their abilities and resilience by joining peer support networks. Peer support networks are an excellent way for service professionals to learn from each other, collaborate, and overcome obstacles together so they can provide clients with outstanding service. The key to perfecting the art of customer service is ultimately understanding how to use peer support networks, which improves the lives of both service providers and the clients they assist.

Team Training and Development

In order to provide service workers with the abilities, information, and frame of mind required to handle challenging situations in the customer service industry with professionalism and ease, team training and development are essential. Providing outstanding customer service has become a crucial distinction for businesses looking to prosper in the cutthroat business environment of today. Beyond technical proficiency, becoming an expert in customer service requires a deep understanding of the needs of the client, effective communication skills, emotional intelligence, and the flexibility to innovate and adjust to the needs of the customer as they change. Initiatives for team training and development give employees the skills and assets they need to succeed in their positions, improve the client experience overall, and foster client loyalty.

Giving service personnel the know-how and abilities to manage a variety of client encounters is one of the main goals of team training and development. Programs for service professionals include themes including active listening, empathy, problem-solving, conflict resolution, and communication tactics. These topics give professionals the tools and strategies they need to handle difficult situations with professionalism and confidence. Training programs enable service workers to interact with clients empathetically, immediately address their concerns, and provide solutions that match their requirements and expectations by imparting these fundamental abilities.

Initiatives for team training and development can help companies cultivate a culture of ongoing learning and development. In order to meet the constantly changing needs of their clients, service providers must adjust and evolve with the times in today's dynamic business climate. Service personnel can stay up to date on industry trends, new technologies, and customer service best practices by enrolling in training programs. Organizations can guarantee that their teams are flexible, strong, and capable of providing outstanding customer service by investing in continuous learning and development.

Initiatives for team training and development also encourage cooperation and teamwork among service providers, creating a safe space where team members can exchange best practices, learn from one another, and play to each other's strengths to handle challenging situations successfully. Service workers build a sense of unity and camaraderie through group activities, role-playing, and cooperative problem-solving exercises. This allows them to collaborate effectively to meet the requirements and challenges of customers. Organizations may optimize the skills and knowledge of their teams by cultivating a culture of cooperation and teamwork, which will improve customer results and experiences.

Apart from providing training on fundamental skills, team training and development programs frequently concentrate on specific aspects of customer service, such managing challenging customers, addressing escalations, or resolving intricate problems. Service professionals can learn sophisticated skills and strategies for handling difficult contacts with professionalism and grace through these focused training programs. Organizations can guarantee that their teams are well-equipped to manage any scenario that may happen during customer contacts, from simple questions to serious escalations, by providing service professionals with specialized skills and knowledge.

Although there are many advantages to team training and development programs for both businesses and service professionals, there are obstacles and factors to take into account when putting them into practice. Making sure that training curricula are in line with corporate aims and objectives and customized to the unique requirements and preferences of service professionals is a problem. It is imperative that training programs are pertinent, captivating, and valuable in order to furnish service personnel with practical knowledge and abilities that they can utilize immediately in their positions. Organizations can optimize the efficiency and influence of their training and development programs by carrying out needs assessments, requesting input, and tailoring training materials to address gaps and priorities.

To ensure the success of team training and development projects, firms must also commit enough resources and support. Time, money, and infrastructure—including technological platforms, facilitators, and training materials—all need to be invested in training programs. Organizations also need to foster a positive learning atmosphere where service workers are inspired to take part in training exercises, use newly acquired skills in their jobs, and get regular coaching and feedback from peers and management. Organizations can show their teams that they value and support their members' professional development by investing in training resources and displaying a commitment to employee development.

In order to determine the efficacy of team training and development programs and pinpoint areas in need of improvement, businesses must also monitor and analyze their results. Key performance indicators can offer essential insights into how training programs affect service quality and performance. Examples of these indicators include employee engagement measures, customer satisfaction ratings, and first-contact resolution rates. Organizations may evaluate the applicability, relevance, and efficacy of training programs by getting input from managers, customers, and participants. Additionally, they can make data-driven decisions with this information to assist them gradually enhance and optimize their training techniques.

To sum up, team building and training are essential to becoming an expert in customer service and handling challenging situations with poise and professionalism. Training programs give service professionals the information, abilities, and mindset they need to succeed in their positions, enabling teams to provide outstanding client experiences that foster customer loyalty and satisfaction. Additionally, training programs help companies develop a culture of creativity, teamwork, and ongoing learning. This allows teams to change and grow in response to the demands and expectations of their clients. The success and longevity of the company are ultimately invested in team training and development, which also improves the lives of service staff and the clients they assist.

Sharing Best Practices and Lessons Learned

In the ever-evolving and demanding world of customer service, sharing best practices and lessons learned is an essential strategy for employees hoping to handle difficult conversations with professionalism and ease. Mastering the art of customer service requires more than just technical proficiency; it requires a continuous process of learning, adjusting, and improving. By sharing best practices and lessons learned, service professionals can gain new insights, handle complicated client encounters with success, and benefit from the collective knowledge and experiences of their peers. This section examines the advantages that customer service brings to companies and service providers, the significance of exchanging best practices and lessons learned, and tactics for fostering a cooperative and knowledge-sharing culture.

It is imperative to exchange best practices and insights to cultivate an innovative and continuous improvement culture within firms. In the dynamic and constantly evolving field of customer service, a solution that is effective one day might be different from the next. Service personnel may stay up to date with emerging technology, changing client expectations, and industry trends by exchanging best practices and lessons learned. Furthermore, by exchanging best practices, service providers can find areas for development, optimize workflows, and put creative solutions into action that improve client outcomes and experiences. Organizations may adjust to shifting consumer demands and market dynamics and prosper by cultivating a culture of innovation and continual improvement.

The chance for service professionals to gain knowledge from one other's experiences and skills is one of the main advantages of exchanging best practices and lessons discovered. The backgrounds, skill sets, and viewpoints of service professionals within a company might vary, and they all provide different perspectives, insights, and methods of providing customer service. Service providers can draw from this collective knowledge base by exchanging best practices, which can provide them with fresh insights, viewpoints, and approaches to handling challenging situations. Service workers can also avoid common traps, foresee obstacles, and negotiate challenging conversations with greater confidence and skill by sharing lessons learned from past experiences, successes, and failures.

Service providers can more easily collaborate and operate as a team to meet the requirements and problems of their clients when they share best practices and lessons learned. Service professionals can benefit from one another's abilities and experience through cross-functional collaboration. By combining different viewpoints and skill sets, they can create novel ideas and solutions for customer service. Organizations may optimize the talents and capabilities of their teams and improve customer experiences and outcomes by cultivating a culture of cooperation and teamwork.

Within organizations, sharing best practices and lessons gained fosters responsibility and openness in addition to creativity and teamwork. When people are honest with their peers about their successes, setbacks, and lessons learned, service providers help to create an environment of accountability where people take ownership of their actions and outcomes. Additionally, by sharing best practices, businesses may discover and replicate success stories, recognize top performers, and celebrate achievements—all of which contribute to the development of a culture that honors and values outstanding customer service. Companies may create a positive and supportive work environment that boosts employee performance and engagement by encouraging accountability and openness among their teams.

Although exchanging best practices and lessons learned has many advantages for businesses and service providers, there are obstacles and issues to be aware of when putting it into effect. Overcoming barriers to knowledge sharing, such as corporate hierarchies, information silos, and cultural aversion to change, is one task. Service industry professionals may be reluctant to impart their wisdom out of concern for criticism, rivalry, or retaliation. Furthermore, organizational procedures and structures may obstruct communication and cooperation, making it challenging for service providers to obtain and efficiently share best practices. By removing these barriers and creating a welcoming environment that values open communication and information sharing, organizations can help their teams reach their maximum potential and enable continuous customer service development.

In order for service professionals to cooperate and exchange knowledge, organizations must also guarantee that they have access to the platforms, tools, and resources they require. Technology is essential for knowledge sharing because it offers platforms for document exchange, project collaboration, discussion boards, and forum participation. To further promote and facilitate information sharing among service providers, companies might put in place formal mechanisms like communities of practice, mentorship programs, and knowledge-sharing sessions. Organizations can develop a culture of cooperation and ongoing learning by investing in the appropriate infrastructure and technology, which will facilitate knowledge exchange and make the process smooth and easy for users.

In conclusion, exchanging best practices and insights is critical to handling challenging situations in the customer service industry with poise and professionalism. Through using the combined knowledge and expertise of their colleagues, customer service representatives can generate fresh perspectives, devise efficient tactics, and promote ongoing enhancement and novelty in the field. Furthermore, the exchange of best practices among firms promotes responsibility, transparency, and teamwork, resulting in a good and encouraging work atmosphere that enhances employee engagement and productivity. In the end, exchanging best practices and lessons learned is an investment in the organization's success and longevity, improving the lives of both service providers and the clients they assist.

CHAPTER X

Continuous Improvement and Feedback

Seeking Customer Feedback

In the ever-changing world of customer service, getting feedback from customers is a critical tactic used by experts to handle challenging situations with poise and expertise. Insights into client perceptions, preferences, and pain points can be gained from customer feedback. This helps service providers find areas for improvement, respond quickly to issues, and provide experiences that both meet and beyond customers' expectations. This section delves into the significance of obtaining client feedback in the context of customer service, the advantages it presents for service providers and organizations, and the methods for efficiently acquiring and utilizing consumer feedback to propel ongoing enhancement and superiority in customer service.

To learn about your clients' wants and objectives, you must solicit their comments. Customer expectations are continuously changing in today's competitive business climate due to a variety of variables, including market trends, shifting consumer behaviours, and technological improvements. Service providers can keep up with these changes, spot new trends and preferences, and modify their service delivery methods by asking clients for input. Additionally, client feedback helps service providers identify areas of improvement and pain spots, allowing them to focus their efforts on those that will have the most significant effects on customer loyalty and happiness.

Getting input from customers helps companies develop a customer-centric culture, which is one of the main advantages of doing so. Organizations may demonstrate to their clients that they value and respect their thoughts and experiences by aggressively seeking out their input. Incorporating customers into the feedback process also gives them the opportunity to express their opinions, raise issues, and help make products and services better. Organizations may develop solid and enduring relationships with their consumers that promote advocacy and loyalty by cultivating an environment of openness and transparency.

In addition, asking for client input helps support staff recognize problems early on and take action before they become more serious. Service providers can identify any issues or pain spots that might be influencing client loyalty and happiness by proactively seeking feedback. Customer feedback offers essential insights into areas that want improvement, whether it's a product failure, a service inconsistency, or a misunderstanding. Service providers can show their dedication to client satisfaction and gain the trust and confidence of their clients by quickly and effectively resolving these problems.

Asking for input from customers not only helps detect and resolve problems but also offers chances for relationship- and service-building. When clients give feedback regarding a lousy encounter or problem, customer care representatives have the opportunity to listen to their worries, offer an apology for any trouble caused, and take action to satisfy the client. A negative experience can be turned into a positive one, winning back the trust and loyalty of customers by service workers responding to complaints and feedback with professionalism and empathy. In addition, asking for feedback enables customer service representatives to follow up with clients following a resolution, guaranteeing that the problem has been entirely resolved and the client is happy with the result.

Although getting client feedback has many advantages for businesses and service providers, there are obstacles and things to think about when putting it into practice. Making sure feedback systems are readily available, intuitive to use, and in line with customer preferences is a problem. Consumers are more inclined to offer feedback when the procedure is easy to use, transparent, and discreet. In addition, companies need to consider the interests and demographics of their clientele and adjust their feedback systems appropriately. Organizations may optimize involvement and satisfy varied customer preferences by providing a range of feedback methods, including social media platforms, online forms, surveys, and comment cards.

It is imperative for organizations to establish protocols and mechanisms that facilitate the effective collection, assessment, and handling of customer feedback. Organizations need more than just gathering feedback; they also need to have systems in place for data analysis and interpretation, trend and pattern identification, and improvement priority ranking. Organizations also need to make sure that input is taken into consideration and that responsibility for putting projects and changes into action is delegated. Organizations may show their dedication to customer satisfaction and continual development by implementing a closed-loop feedback approach, which will improve customer outcomes and experiences.

Organizations also need to encourage a culture of continual development and feedback among their teams. It is essential to enable service providers to ask clients for feedback on a proactive basis, to listen to their complaints actively, and to take responsibility for fixing problems and promoting changes. Additionally, companies should offer opportunities for training and development so that service workers may improve their empathy, problem-solving, and communication skills, which will help them handle challenging situations with professionalism and ease. Organizations may establish an environment where service workers feel empowered to provide excellent service experiences that surpass customer expectations by cultivating a culture of feedback and continual improvement.

In summary, getting feedback from customers is an essential tactic for handling challenging situations in the customer service industry with poise and expertise. Service providers may identify areas for improvement, quickly address issues, and provide experiences that encourage customer satisfaction and loyalty by asking for and receiving feedback from customers. This enables them to gather crucial information about the needs, preferences, and problems of their clients. In addition, asking for feedback helps companies develop a customer-focused culture, increases customer trust and confidence, and opens doors for relationship- and service-building. In the end, asking for customer feedback is an investment in the organization's success and longevity, improving the lives of both customer service representatives and the clients they assist.

Reflecting on Interactions for Growth

For customer service workers who want to handle challenging situations with professionalism and ease, reflecting on encounters for growth is an essential habit.

Every engagement in the fast-paced, dynamic field of customer service offers a chance for development, learning, and progress. Through reflective practises, service professionals can get significant insights into their customer interactions, pinpoint areas of improvement, and enhance their abilities and methodologies to provide outstanding service experiences. This section examines the value of reflection in customer service, the advantages it offers for businesses and service professionals, and practical methods for incorporating reflection into day-to-day operations to promote excellence and ongoing development in customer service.

Service providers can better understand their strengths, shortcomings, and opportunities for development by reflecting on encounters. In order to fulfil the requirements and expectations of their customers, service professionals must be able to adapt and respond effectively to the unique difficulties and possibilities that each client engagement brings. Service providers can evaluate their performance, pinpoint areas of strength and weakness, and discover places where they may have gone short by reflecting on their encounters. Additionally, through introspection, service providers can learn more about their interpersonal abilities, communication styles, and emotional intelligence. This knowledge helps them create plans for improving their efficacy and professionalism in future encounters.

The ability of reflection to promote self-awareness and personal development is one of its main advantages. Service professionals can better understand their motivations, values, and behaviours by reflecting on their work. This helps them to make decisions that are consistent with their objectives and goals for their career. Furthermore, by reflecting on their encounters, service providers might spot patterns and trends that help them identify reoccurring problems or concerns that might need addressing. Service providers can adopt a growth mentality by working on their self-awareness. This mindset sees every interaction as a chance for learning and improvement rather than as a cause for aggravation or disappointment.

Reflecting on encounters also helps firms develop an innovative and continuous improvement culture. Organizations foster chances for collective learning and growth by enabling service professionals to reflect on their encounters and share their ideas with their colleagues. Through venues for information exchange, peer feedback sessions, and group conversations, service professionals can get fresh insights, learn from one another's experiences, and create creative solutions to shared problems. Organizations can also make data-driven decisions and execute focused actions to enhance service delivery by using reflection to find trends and patterns in customer feedback.

Reflecting on interactions helps service professionals not only grow personally but also enhance their organization by assisting them to forge stronger bonds with their clients. Service providers can adjust their approach to match each customer's unique expectations by reflecting on their interactions to obtain insights into the preferences, needs, and motivations of their clients. Additionally, via reflection, service providers can spot chances to establish connection, empathy, and trust with their clients, improving the client experience in general and encouraging advocacy and long-term loyalty. Customer satisfaction and self-improvement are two ways that service providers can develop long-lasting relationships with their consumers and boost referrals and repeat business.

Though there are many advantages to reflection for businesses and service providers, there are obstacles and things to keep in mind when putting it into practice.

Finding the time and space for introspection among the rigours and stresses of everyday employment is one challenge. In the hectic and pressure-filled world of customer service, employees may find it difficult to stop and think back on their encounters. Service providers may also be reluctant to reflect because they are uncomfortable with introspection or fear judgment or self-criticism. Organizations can help service professionals emphasize self-reflection as a crucial component of their daily practice by setting aside time and place for it.

Organizations also need to supply tools and assistance so that service professionals can adequately participate in reflection. Peer support groups, coaching sessions, and training programs can give service workers the methods, strategies, and direction they require to participate in meaningful reflection. Organizations can also use technology to encourage introspection by offering digital tools and platforms for goal-setting, journaling, and self-evaluation. Organizations can enable service professionals to take charge of their own personal and professional growth and promote excellence in customer service by offering resources and support for reflection.

To sum up, service professionals who want to handle challenging situations in the field of customer service with professionalism and ease must engage in the essential practice of reflecting on encounters for growth. Service providers can enhance their interactions, pinpoint areas for development, and hone their techniques to provide excellent service experiences by reflecting on their experiences. Reflection also promotes self-awareness, individual growth, and organizational advancement, which propels ongoing innovation and customer service improvement. Organizations can foster a culture of learning, development, and excellence that benefits both service workers and the clients they serve by incorporating reflection into everyday operations.

Iterative Learning and Development

To become an expert in customer service and handle challenging situations with professionalism and ease, one must engage in iterative learning and improvement. Customer service representatives work in a fast-paced, dynamic industry where they must constantly improve and adjust their methods, approaches, and tactics to suit the ever-changing needs and expectations of customers. Through a cycle of learning, experimentation, reflection, and refinement, iterative learning and development helps service professionals get better at what they do, spur innovation, and provide outstanding customer experiences. This section explores the benefits of iterative learning and development, the advantages it offers to businesses and service providers, and doable ways to integrate it into everyday operations with the goal of fostering excellence in customer service and continuous improvement. In order to promote excellence in customer service and continuous improvement, this section examines the advantages of iterative learning and development, as well as the benefits it brings to companies and service providers. It also looks at practical ways to incorporate it into daily operations.

Through constant experimenting and learning, service professionals strive to determine what works and what doesn't through trial and error in iterative learning and development. Service workers can learn more about various approaches, techniques, and strategies and their effects on customer interactions by trying them out. Additionally, service providers can test theories, verify presumptions, and investigate novel approaches to providing value to clients through experimentation. Service providers can find novel approaches to everyday problems, hone their abilities, and spot chances for development and advancement by trying new things.

Iterative learning and development's ability to foster innovation and ongoing organizational improvement is one of its main advantages. Service professionals that work for companies that encourage experimentation and iteration are able to try out new concepts, take measured risks, and question the status quo. Iterative learning and development also helps companies rapidly get used to shifting market conditions and client demands. Service providers that cultivate an atmosphere that emphasizes agility, flexibility, and resilience inside their companies may be able to stay ahead of the competition and provide great client experiences that increase customer satisfaction and loyalty. One way to achieve this is by encouraging service providers to innovate and try new things.

Additionally, iterative learning and development help service professionals adopt a growth mindset by empowering them to see obstacles and failures as chances for personal improvement. Customer service representatives usually deal with a variety of challenging situations. Service providers who adopt a growth mindset may meet these obstacles with curiosity, hope, and fortitude because they understand that every encounter is a chance for personal development. Furthermore, service workers can learn from mistakes and setbacks quickly and use them as valuable lessons to guide future actions and decisions thanks to iterative learning and development.

Iterative learning and development not only promotes a growth mindset and continual progress but also helps service workers become more resilient and adaptable when faced with challenges. Service providers frequently deal with challenging encounters in their work, such as managing high-stress situations, confronting furious consumers, and resolving complex difficulties. The skills and talents needed to handle these problems with professionalism and ease can be developed by service professionals through iterative learning and development. Furthermore, service professionals can acquire resilience and adaptability over time through iterative learning and development, which gives them the tools they need to flourish in the face of ambiguity, change, and uncertainty.

Although there are many advantages to iterative learning and development for companies and service providers, there are obstacles and factors to take into account when putting it into practice. Establishing a welcoming atmosphere that promotes experimentation and iteration is one issue. Efficiency and risk aversion may be valued more highly in some firms than creativity and exploration. Service providers may also be afraid to try new things or take chances for fear of failing or facing consequences. By encouraging a culture that encourages experimenting, learning, and taking risks, organizations may help service professionals incorporate iterative learning and growth into their daily work.

Iterative learning and development programs also require the resources and support that businesses have to offer in order to be successful. Workshops, coaching sessions, and training programs can give service professionals the methods, strategies, and direction they need to experiment and iterate successfully. Additionally, by providing service professionals access to technology and data analytics tools, firms may help them gather, examine, and understand performance data and feedback in order to guide their learning and development initiatives better. Organizations can enable service professionals to take charge of their own personal and professional development and promote excellence in customer service by offering resources and support for iterative learning and development.

To sum up, learning and improvement through iteration are crucial to becoming an expert in customer service and handling challenging situations with poise and professionalism. Service providers may consistently enhance their performance, spur innovation, and provide outstanding customer experiences by adopting an experimentation and iteration culture. Additionally, iterative learning and development help service workers create a growth mindset, resilience, and adaptability so they can flourish in the face of unpredictability and hardship. Organizations can foster a culture of learning, development, and excellence that benefits both service professionals and the clients they serve by incorporating iterative learning and development into routine operations.

CHAPTER XI

Personal Well-being and Self-Care

Managing Stress and Burnout

Managing stress and burnout is crucial for customer service professionals who want to handle challenging contacts with professionalism and ease in the demanding and high-pressure world of customer service. Working in customer service positions frequently entails tackling a variety of difficulties, such as managing irate clients or addressing complicated problems, all while attempting to fulfil strict performance goals and service standards. As a result, employees in the service sector are more susceptible to high stress and burnout levels, which can have a detrimental effect on their wellness, performance, and ability to deliver exceptional customer experiences. This section examines the significance of stress and burnout management in the customer service industry, the causes of stress and burnout in the industry, and practical approaches to stress and burnout management that support customer service excellence and resilience.

Preserving the wellbeing and mental health of those working in the service industry requires effective management of stress and burnout. The rigorous demands of customer service positions, in addition to ongoing pressure to fulfil performance goals and client expectations, can be detrimental to the mental and emotional wellbeing of service personnel. The long-term effects of burnout and chronic stress include weariness, exhaustion, irritability, and decreased job satisfaction. Furthermore, a protracted period of elevated stress might raise the chance of developing more severe health conditions like anxiety, depression, and cardiovascular disease. Service providers can safeguard their mental and emotional health, preserve their resilience, and continue to perform and be effective in their professions by proactively managing stress and burnout.

The rigorous and emotionally taxing nature of customer interactions is one of the leading causes of stress and burnout among service professionals. Managing demanding circumstances, finding solutions to challenging issues, and soothing irate clients can be physically and psychologically exhausting. Furthermore, the stress and burnout experienced by service workers can be exacerbated by contradictory demands, unreasonable expectations, and ongoing oversight from management and customers. Moreover, it can be challenging for customer service representatives to unplug and refuel due to the fast-paced and unpredictable nature of their jobs, which can result in feelings of overload and tiredness. Service providers can create plans for lessening the effects of stress and burnout and preserving their wellbeing by knowing what causes them.

In addition, the work environment and corporate culture have a significant impact on how stressed and burned-out service workers become. There may exist a culture of overwork in certain firms, when service professionals are expected to put in long hours, shoulder heavy workloads, and put production ahead of their own wellbeing. Organizational structures and procedures can also lead to stress and burnout by limiting autonomy and decision-making power, establishing a competitive environment, and putting pressure on employees to perform well. The issue may also be made worse by a lack of training opportunities, employee support programs, mental health resources, and other tools for managing stress and burnout. Service providers are less likely to experience anxiety and burnout when working in an inclusive, supportive atmosphere that puts employee wellbeing first. This also helps to provide the circumstances necessary for consistent performance and effectiveness.

Furthermore, in order to effectively manage stress and burnout, service professionals must learn resilience-building methods and coping mechanisms for the demands and complexities of their jobs. People can manage stress and enhance their mental health by practicing mindfulness and relaxation techniques like yoga, meditation, and deep breathing exercises. Setting limits and creating a work-life balance can also help service providers. Some examples of these practices include scheduling frequent breaks, defining reasonable goals, and assigning work as needed. In addition, creating social support networks and asking for help from peers, mentors, and managers can give service providers the support, direction, and understanding they require to manage stress and handle challenging situations.

Individual coping mechanisms are crucial for handling stress and burnout, but companies also have an obligation to promote employee wellbeing and foster a resilient workplace culture. Employers can support their employees' mental and emotional health in a number of ways, such as by providing them with employee assistance programs, mental health resources, and counseling services. Organizations can also support work-life balance by providing workshops on stress management, wellness initiatives, and flexible work schedules. Organizations should also encourage a culture of open communication, constructive criticism, and assistance so that service providers are at ease sharing their difficulties and asking for help when necessary. Organizations can lessen the likelihood of stress and burnout among service professionals and improve their capacity to provide outstanding customer experiences by putting an emphasis on employee wellbeing and fostering a supportive work environment.

In conclusion, service professionals who want to handle challenging situations in the field of customer service with expertise and ease must learn how to manage stress and burnout. Service professionals can safeguard their wellbeing, retain their effectiveness, and continue to perform in their roles by comprehending the elements that lead to anxiety and burnout, creating coping mechanisms and resilience-building techniques, and cultivating a supportive work environment. Furthermore, corporations are essential in fostering resilience and wellbeing within their workforce as well as supporting their mental and emotional wellbeing. Organizations may lower the risk of stress and burnout among service professionals and improve their capacity to provide outstanding client experiences by putting an emphasis on employee wellbeing and fostering a culture of wellness and support.

Practicing Self-Compassion

In order to handle challenging situations in the customer service industry with professionalism and ease, self-compassion practice is essential. In order to fulfil strict performance standards and customer expectations, customer service positions frequently entail managing difficult situations, such as processing complaints, settling disputes, and managing high-stress interactions. Service providers may feel higher levels of stress, self-criticism, and burnout in such demanding settings. In order to practice self-compassion, one must be kind, understanding, and accepting of oneself when facing challenges and disappointments. In order to improve wellbeing, resilience, and efficacy in customer service, this section examines the value of self-compassion practice, the advantages it provides for service providers and organizations, and practical methods for incorporating self-compassion into day-to-day operations.

Protecting service workers' mental health and general wellbeing in the demanding field of customer care requires them to engage in self-compassion practices. The mental and emotional well-being of service professionals can be negatively impacted by the ongoing pressure to fulfil performance goals, handle difficult situations, and keep their cool. Moreover, when confronted with challenging circumstances or disappointments, service professionals may feel inadequate, perfectionist, and self-critical. Service providers can develop a loving and caring internal dialogue and offset self-criticism with kindness and understanding by engaging in self-compassion practices. Furthermore, self-compassion helps care providers to accept and be resilient in the face of hardship by allowing them to talk about their flaws and challenges without passing judgment.

The ability of self-compassion practice to promote emotional resilience and wellbeing among service providers is one of its main advantages. Workers in customer service positions regularly deal with high levels of stress, annoyance, and criticism from clients and coworkers. Service providers may also come across challenging situations that cause them to feel angry, anxious, or self-conscious. Service providers can cultivate the abilities and skills necessary to successfully control their emotional responses, manage their stress levels, and recover more quickly and resiliently from setbacks by engaging in self-compassion practices. Furthermore, even in the face of difficult situations, service providers can develop an inner sense of calm and well-being by practising self-compassion.

Moreover, engaging in self-compassion practices helps service providers keep a positive outlook on their performance and tasks. Customer service representatives may feel pressure to deliver excellent work in the fast-paced and demanding field constantly. Furthermore, comparisons to peers or unattainable perfection standards can cause feelings of inadequacy or self-doubt in service professions. Service providers can have a more realistic and balanced view of their skills, accomplishments, and limitations by engaging in self- compassion practices. Furthermore, by practising self- compassion, service providers can see that their errors and mistakes are a regular aspect of learning rather than a reflection of their value or skill.

Furthermore, engaging in self-compassion practices helps service providers handle challenging situations and settle disputes in a relaxed, collected manner. Employees in customer service positions frequently
face challenging circumstances that need emotional intelligence, empathy, and patience to handle. In addition, service providers may encounter animosity, violence, or criticism from patrons, which makes it challenging to remain composed and professional. Service providers can develop resilience and inner serenity by engaging in self-compassion practices.This will enable them to respond to difficult circumstances with poise, understanding, and clarity. When service providers are self-compassionate, they may also approach challenging situations with an attitude of openness and curiosity instead of defensiveness or reactivity, which results in more positive and productive outcomes for all parties.

While self-compassion practises provide numerous benefits for organizations and service providers, there are certain challenges and considerations that must be made while implementing them. Overcoming social and cultural barriers to self-compassion, such as the stigma associated with weakness, vulnerability, or self-care, is one problem. Instead of being seen as an essential trait for resilience and well-being, self-compassion may be seen in some cultures or organizations as a sign of weakness or self-indulgence. Furthermore, service industry workers could be reluctant to engage in self-compassion exercises out of concern for their peers' or managers' opinions or judgments. Organizations can foster an inclusive and encouraging atmosphere that prioritizes resilience and wellbeing by educating and training individuals in self-compassion strategies and increasing awareness of the significance of self-compassion.

Organizations can also take steps to encourage a culture of compassion and care and support service providers in practising self-compassion. The skills, methods, and direction required for service professionals to develop self-compassion in their everyday lives can be given through training courses, seminars, and coaching sessions. Organizations can also encourage self-care and well-being by providing tools like stress management classes, mindfulness exercises, and relaxation methods. Organizations can also promote a collaborative and supportive peer culture where service professionals are at ease discussing difficulties, asking for assistance when necessary, and lending support to one another. Organizations may foster an environment where service professionals flourish and provide outstanding client experiences by placing a high priority on self-compassion and wellbeing.

In conclusion, developing self-compassion is an essential ability for customer service representatives who want to handle challenging situations in the field with poise and professionalism. Serving others and being kind, understanding, and accepting of oneself are ways that service workers can safeguard their health, build their resilience, and continue to thrive in their positions. Furthermore, the ability to be self-compassionate helps service providers maintain a good outlook on their work and performance, handle challenging situations with understanding and grace, and create favourable outcomes for both themselves and their clients. Organizations can establish a compassionate and caring culture and incorporate self-compassion into daily operations to enable service workers to flourish and provide excellent client experiences that surpass expectations.

Balancing Work and Life Demands

Learning how to manage work and personal obligations is essential to becoming a skilled customer service provider and handling challenging situations with poise and professionalism. Service professionals frequently have to handle heavy workloads, meet deadlines, and juggle many tasks while trying to provide clients with extraordinary service experiences in today's fast- paced and competitive corporate climate. Yet, the ongoing pressure to produce outstanding work can be detrimental to employees' health in the service sector by raising stress levels, leading to burnout, and decreasing job satisfaction. This section examines the significance of striking a balance between work and personal obligations for customer service representatives, the obstacles they encounter in doing so, and practical methods for handling work-life balance in a way that improves resilience, well-being, well-being, and performance in customer service positions.

In the demanding world of customer service, maintaining a healthy work-life balance is crucial to protecting service workers' physical, mental, and emotional health. Due to the demands of clients and corporate operations, service professionals frequently put in long hours, especially on the weekends, holidays, and in the evenings. Service providers may also feel pressure to reply to questions from clients and address problems as soon as possible, even outside regular business hours. Because of this, service workers could find it challenging to take a break from their jobs, refuel, and partake in activities that enhance well-being, such as hanging out with friends and family, taking up a hobby, or practising self-care. Service professionals can safeguard their health, keep up their energy levels, and continue to perform and be effective in their professions by striking a balance between work and home life.

Keeping a clear separation between work and personal life is one of the biggest obstacles facing service industry workers in their quest for work-life balance. Service personnel may experience pressure in their customer service professions to be available and responsive to customers at all times, including during their own time. Service workers may also encounter demands from supervisors or peers to work extended shifts or take on extra duties, which can make it challenging to set limits and put one's own needs first. Service providers may also feel guilty or anxious about taking time off from work or placing restrictions on their availability because they worry about coming across as unprofessional or uncommitted. Service providers may make time for leisure, relaxation, and renewal by setting up clear boundaries between their personal and professional lives. This will allow them to refuel and give their all in their work.

Additionally, in order to achieve work-life balance, service industry workers must make self-care and well-being a priority in their day-to-day activities. Customer service representatives may put the demands of their clients and company operations ahead of their own needs in the stressful environment of customer service. On the other hand, skipping out on self-care can result in burnout, diminished job satisfaction, and mental and physical tiredness. Prioritizing self-care activities helps service workers refuel, lower stress levels, and become more resilient in the face of adversity. These practices include regular exercise, a balanced diet, enough sleep, and stress management skills. In addition, taking care of oneself helps service providers stay optimistic, encourage originality and creativity, and stay motivated and involved in their work.

In order to attain a work-life balance, service industry professionals must also establish clear guidelines, use time management techniques, and assign work as needed. It can be challenging for service personnel in customer service professions to successfully manage their workload and prioritize assignments since they frequently have to deal with conflicting demands and priorities. Additionally, in order to achieve deadlines or surpass performance goals, service workers can experience pressure to multitask or put in longer hours, which could result in feelings of overload and burnout. Service providers can make room for concentrated work, prevent burnout, and attain a better sense of balance and control over their workload by defining priorities, creating clear boundaries, and assigning duties to coworkers or superiors. In addition, proficient time management allows service providers to schedule personal and work-related activities, guaranteeing that they have time for rest, relaxation, and renewal.

While achieving work-life balance offers businesses and service providers numerous benefits, there are challenges and considerations to make when putting it into practice. Overcoming organizational and cultural impediments to work-life balance, such as the belief that putting in long hours or forgoing personal time is essential for success or progress, is one problem. There may be a culture of overwork in some companies, where workers are expected to put work before their personal lives and show steadfast dedication to their jobs. Furthermore, work-life balance may be discouraged by organizational structures and procedures that restrict individuals' freedom, autonomy, and ability to prioritize and meet their own needs. Organizations can foster an inclusive and encouraging work environment that prioritizes and supports employee well-being by questioning these cultural norms and supporting work-life balance efforts.

In addition, maintaining a healthy work-life balance necessitates that service industry workers speak up for themselves and effectively convey their needs to supervisors and peers. Fearing that they would come across as unprofessional or uncommitted, service professionals in customer service professions may be reluctant to set boundaries, request time off, or discuss their personal priorities with superiors or coworkers. Nonetheless, mutual understanding and cooperation between service providers and their peers or supervisors depend on open communication and transparency. Service workers can get a better work-life balance and overall well-being by proactively conveying their requirements, preferences, and limitations to their colleagues. This builds mutual respect, trust, and support.

In conclusion, finding a work-life balance is crucial for professionals in the service industry who want to handle challenging situations in the field of customer care with professionalism and ease. Service professionals can safeguard their health, preserve their energy, and continue to perform and be effective in their roles by managing the boundary between work and personal life, prioritizing self-care and well-being, setting boundaries, and communicating needs in an effective manner. In addition, companies have a vital role to play in fostering work-life balance by encouraging employee well-being, flexibility, and autonomy. Organizations may foster a culture of resilience, creativity, and engagement that benefits both service providers and the clients they serve by placing a high priority on work-life balance and employee well-being.

CHAPTER XII

Case Studies and Real-Life Scenarios

Analyzing Successful Resolutions

Understanding how to analyze successful outcomes is essential to being an expert in customer service and handling challenging situations with poise and expertise. Service providers face a wide range of difficulties in the ever-changing world of customer service, from managing complaints to finding solutions for complicated problems while upholding strict service standards. In addition to satisfying clients, effective remedies enhance the organization's reputation and promote trust and loyalty. This section examines the significance of dissecting effective customer service resolutions, the essential elements of such resolutions, and methods by which service providers can improve their resolution abilities in order to provide outstanding client experiences.

Effective customer service resolutions involve more than just taking care of the immediate issue; they also include building strong bonds with the clients. Understanding the demands of the consumer, feeling their problems, and coming up with workable solutions that either match or surpass their expectations are all necessary for a successful resolution. Additionally, open communication, honesty, and follow-up are essential for successful resolutions in order to guarantee that the client feels appreciated and supported at every stage of the procedure. Service providers can learn the methods and approaches that produce favourable results by dissecting successful resolutions. This will help them repeat similar accomplishments in subsequent interactions.

Good problem-solving abilities are essential for successful resolutions. Service providers need to be able to determine and comprehend the underlying reason for the customer's problem, evaluate pertinent data, and offer workable solutions that deal with the underlying issue. Service providers also need to be imaginative, adaptable, and inventive in their search for solutions that satisfy the distinct requirements and preferences of every client. Service providers can enhance their problem-solving abilities and provide more impactful solutions in subsequent interactions by examining successful resolutions to detect patterns, trends, and best practices.

Moreover, effective responses necessitate that service providers have excellent interpersonal and communication abilities. Active listening, empathy, and clarity in information delivery and customer service are all necessary for effective communication. Furthermore, even in difficult situations, service providers need to be skilled at controlling their emotions, calming heated situations, and acting professionally. Service personnel can improve their communication skills and establish connections with clients by identifying communication methods and techniques that result in positive outcomes through the analysis of successful resolutions.

Successful resolutions also require cooperation and coordination inside the company. Service providers need to collaborate closely with coworkers, managers, and other departments in order to obtain data, plan answers, and successfully execute solutions. In order to efficiently address client concerns, service providers must also make use of internal resources, including knowledge bases, training materials, and support systems. These resources give them access to pertinent information and expertise. Service providers can find chances for internal synergy and collaboration by examining successful resolutions. This allows them to make better use of internal resources and provide better results for their clients.

Furthermore, service providers need to be resilient and adaptive in the face of obstacles and failures in order for resolutions to be successful. Managing stressful situations, facing unforeseen barriers, and addressing challenging conversations are all everyday responsibilities in customer service professions. Resilience is a quality that service workers must possess. This includes picking up lessons from mistakes and setbacks, changing course when necessary, and recovering from them swiftly. Service providers can find resilience-building methods and approaches that help them stay calm, self-assured, and productive in trying circumstances by examining successful resolutions.

While researching effective solutions has numerous benefits for businesses and service providers, there are challenges and considerations when implementing them. The availability and calibre of data for analysis present one difficulty. Large volumes of data are produced by customer service interactions, including comments from customers, service requests, and the results of resolutions. However, successfully gathering, organizing, and analyzing this data may prove difficult for businesses, which may hinder their capacity to draw valuable conclusions and spot successful trends. Organizations can improve their ability to examine successful resolutions and use data-driven insights to improve performance and outcomes by investing in data analytics tools and training programs.

Additionally, examining effective resolutions necessitates an organizational culture that values ongoing learning and development. In order to improve their knowledge and abilities, service professionals should be encouraged to think back on their experiences, collaborate with peers to share best practices and insights, and take part in training and development initiatives. Organizations also need to give service workers the tools and resources they need to practice reflectively, like peer support groups, coaching, and mentoring. By fostering a learning and development culture, organizations can empower service professionals to evaluate successful responses and encourage continuous customer service improvement.

To sum up, understanding effective resolution techniques is crucial to becoming a skilled customer care agent and handling challenging situations with poise and composure. Service professionals can improve their resolution skills and provide outstanding customer experiences by knowing the essential elements of successful resolutions, such as problem-solving abilities, interpersonal and communication skills, cooperation and teamwork, resilience, and adaptability. Customer loyalty, trust, and contentment will all increase when a culture of constant learning and development is established. Organizations can also empower service staff to analyze effective solutions and encourage constant customer service improvement.

Learning from Mistakes and Challenges

A key component of perfecting the art of customer service and handling challenging situations with professionalism and ease is learning from mistakes and setbacks. The dynamic and demanding world of customer service presents a wide range of problems for service professionals, from managing high-stress situations and reaching performance standards to dealing with complaints and resolving disagreements. In any customer service position, errors and difficulties are unavoidable, but they also offer priceless chances for development, education, and advancement. This section examines the value of learning from customer service mishaps and setbacks, the advantages it provides for service providers and businesses, and practical methods for utilizing mishaps and setbacks to improve performance, resilience, and customer happiness.

Customer service errors and difficulties offer essential insights into areas for development and improvement. Service providers can pinpoint underlying problems, underlying causes, and areas for skill, process, and system development by evaluating errors and difficulties. Errors and problems also highlight gaps in knowledge, problem-solving ability, and communication, which encourages service providers to seek solutions, acquire new skills, and further their careers in order to offer clients more substantial support. A mindset of continual innovation and improvement can be fostered by service professionals by accepting mistakes and problems as teaching opportunities. This will lead to positive transformation and advancement in their professions.

In customer service roles, resilience and flexibility are developed as a result of learning from mistakes and setbacks. Managing stressful situations, facing unforeseen barriers, and addressing challenging conversations are all everyday responsibilities in customer service professions. Service professionals' resilience can be put to the test by mistakes and challenges that force them to step outside of their comfort zones, question their preconceptions, and face their limitations. Service providers can, however, cultivate the resilience to recover from setbacks rapidly, draw lessons from their experiences, and modify their strategy as necessary to produce better results in subsequent interactions by learning from their mistakes and problems.

Moreover, a culture of accountability, ownership, and continuous improvement is fostered within firms via learning from mistakes and problems. Service providers need to own up to their mistakes, own up to their acts, and take aggressive measures to correct them and keep them from happening again. Organizations must also give service personnel the tools and resources they need to grow from their mistakes, including coaching, training courses, and feedback systems. Organizations may empower service workers to own up to their mistakes, learn from them, and be part of the overall improvement of customer service effectiveness and quality by fostering a supportive atmosphere that values transparency, honesty, and learning.

Furthermore, service workers can strengthen their critical thinking and problem-solving skills by learning from their mistakes and problems. In order to effectively meet the demands and concerns of customers, service professionals must frequently think creatively, assess complex circumstances, and offer unique solutions in response to mistakes and problems. In addition, errors and difficulties give service providers the chance to try out new methods, test alternative approaches, and improve their plans in response to input and results. Service providers can enhance their problem-solving abilities and become more productive and resourceful in their professions by accepting mistakes and obstacles as chances for learning and development.

Though there are many advantages for service providers and organizations in learning from mistakes and setbacks, there are obstacles and factors to take into account when putting this strategy into practice. Overcoming the fear of failing and the shame attached to making errors in customer service professions is one issue. Service providers may be reluctant to try new things, take chances, or own up to their mistakes for fear of being judged, criticized, or facing unfavourable outcomes. Furthermore, companies could maintain a culture of punishment and blame where errors are seen as failures rather than chances for growth and development. Creating an environment where psychological safety, openness, and learning are valued might assist service providers in viewing obstacles and failures as chances for development and creativity.

Service providers must adopt a growth mindset and be receptive to learning from their errors if they are to improve as a result of their mishaps and challenges. Rather than seeing errors and setbacks as evidence of one's incapacity or weakness, a growth mindset sees them as chances for learning, development, and improvement. Furthermore, in order to learn from their mistakes, ask for criticism from others, and reflect on their experiences in order to derive important lessons, service professionals need to cultivate self-awareness and humility. By adopting a growth mindset and learning orientation, service professionals can transform setbacks and challenges into chances for both professional and personal development, increasing their efficacy and resilience in customer service roles.

To sum up, developing the skill of providing excellent customer service and handling challenging situations with poise and professionally requires learning from errors and setbacks. Accepting failures and setbacks as opportunities for growth, learning, and advancement can help service providers develop the resilience, critical thinking, and problem-solving abilities required to excel in their roles. Additionally, companies can establish an environment where service professionals are empowered to learn from their errors, enhance the general effectiveness and quality of customer service, and ultimately provide extraordinary customer experiences by cultivating a culture of accountability, ownership, and continuous improvement.

Applying Lessons to Future Interactions

Understanding the art of customer service and handling challenging situations with professionalism and ease requires applying lessons learnt from previous contacts to future ones. In their work, customer service representatives deal with a wide range of issues, from managing high-stress circumstances and satisfying customers' expectations to processing complaints and settling disputes. Every contact is a chance for learning and development for service professionals, who gain knowledge, pinpoint areas for growth, and devise plans to increase their efficacy. This section examines the value of learning from past experiences to improve customer service encounters in the future, as well as the advantages it provides for companies and service professionals. It also offers ways for utilizing prior experiences to navigate challenging situations with competence and confidence successfully.

An essential advantage of using lessons learned in subsequent contacts is being able to foresee and proactively handle possible problems. Service personnel can expect similar scenarios in the future by reflecting on past contacts and identifying reoccurring issues, patterns, and trends. Service providers can also create plans and strategies to reduce risks, stop problems from getting worse, and produce better results. Service workers should approach future contacts with better foresight, preparedness, and confidence by putting the lessons they've learned from past interactions to use. This will help them negotiate challenging situations with professionalism and ease.

Applying lessons learned to new interactions also helps firms develop a culture of ongoing learning and development. To improve their abilities and output, service personnel need to be proactive in seeking out feedback, implementing new insights, and learning from their experiences. Organizations can also encourage and assist service personnel to think back on previous encounters, impart knowledge to peers, and take part in training and development initiatives. Organizations may enable service workers to effectively apply lessons learned to future interactions by fostering a culture that appreciates and encourages learning and growth. This will lead to positive change and advancement in the quality and effectiveness of customer service.

Furthermore, by using what they have learned in subsequent interactions, service workers can improve their interpersonal and communication abilities. In customer service encounters, rapport-building, expectation management, and dispute resolution all depend on effective communication. Service providers can pinpoint communication tactics and approaches that produce favourable results—like active listening, empathy, and precise information delivery—by thinking back on previous exchanges. Service providers can also improve their communication style in response to input and results, which will help them forge closer bonds with clients and coworkers and settle disputes more amicably in the future.

Though there are many advantages for service providers and organizations in using lessons learned in subsequent contacts, there are obstacles and things to keep in mind when putting them into practice. The availability and calibre of data for analysis present one difficulty. Large volumes of data are produced by customer service interactions, including comments from customers, service requests, and the results of resolutions. However, successfully gathering, organizing, and analyzing this data may prove difficult for businesses, which may hinder their capacity to draw valuable conclusions and spot successful trends. Organizations may increase their ability to examine historical interactions and use data-driven insights to improve performance and outcomes by investing in data analytics tools and training programs.

Moreover, in order to incorporate the lessons learned into subsequent contacts, service professionals must cultivate a development mindset and be open to gaining knowledge from their experiences. Rather than seeing errors and setbacks as evidence of incapacity or failure, a growth mentality sees them as chances for development. Service providers also need to learn the humility and self-awareness to accept their own limitations, ask for and receive feedback from others, and think back on their experiences in order to draw vital lessons and insights. In order to improve their efficacy and resilience in customer service roles, service professionals can turn prior experiences into chances for personal and professional development by adopting a growth mindset and a learning orientation.

To sum up, learning from past experiences is crucial to becoming an expert in customer service and handling challenging situations with poise and professionalism. Through introspection, pinpointing shortcomings, and formulating tactics for refinement, customer service representatives can enter future encounters with more awareness, readiness, and self-assurance. Organizations can also establish an environment where service workers are empowered to implement lessons learned in an efficient manner, leading to positive change and advancement in the efficacy and quality of customer service. This can be accomplished through fostering an environment that values ongoing education and development.

CONCLUSION

We started a thorough investigation into the complex field of customer service, finding priceless knowledge and techniques to deal with difficult situations. During this trip, we explored a variety of aspects of exceptional customer service, such as empathy, active listening, problem-solving, and resilience, giving service providers the skills and strategies they need to handle challenging situations with assurance and competence.

As we come to an end, it is clear that developing an attitude of constant improvement, flexibility, and empathy is more important for mastering the art of customer service than simply adhering to a set of strict rules or procedures. Service providers should view every engagement as a chance for growth and learning, using both achievements and failures to hone abilities and boost productivity.

The value of empathy in customer service encounters is one of the book's main lessons. Service providers can have more meaningful and powerful encounters with customers if they put themselves in their customers' shoes and have a deeper understanding of their requirements, problems, and emotions. Furthermore, developing rapport, settling disputes, and cultivating trust are all made possible by active listening and efficient communication, which provide the groundwork for positive results.

We also looked at the importance of resilience in the face of difficulty. Managing unanticipated obstacles, dealing with challenging customers, and navigating high-stress situations are common tasks in customer service professions. Service providers may overcome obstacles, remain calm under duress, and stay committed to providing outstanding customer experiences by developing resilience.

Furthermore, it has been determined that organizational culture and support are essential for promoting service excellence. Organizations must prioritize training and development programs, devote resources to skill upgrading, and foster a culture that supports and fosters continuous learning and growth. Creating a welcoming and supportive work atmosphere for customer service representatives can assist businesses in boosting customer satisfaction, retention, and, ultimately, financial success.

To sum up, "Customer Care Chronicles: Navigating Difficult Interactions with Ease: Mastering the Art of Customer Service" offers a thorough manual and road map for those working in customer service who want to be the best at their jobs. Service professionals can navigate the complexities of customer interactions with grace, professionalism, and effectiveness by embracing empathy, communication, resilience, and continuous learning. In the end, they will be able to deliver exceptional service experiences that have a lasting impact on customers and propel organizational success in today's competitive landscape.

Thank you for buying and reading/ listening to our book. If you found this book useful/ helpful please take a few minutes and leave a review on the platform where you purchased our book. Your feedback matters greatly to us.